Arthur Wesley Dow

AND AMERICAN ARTS & CRAFTS

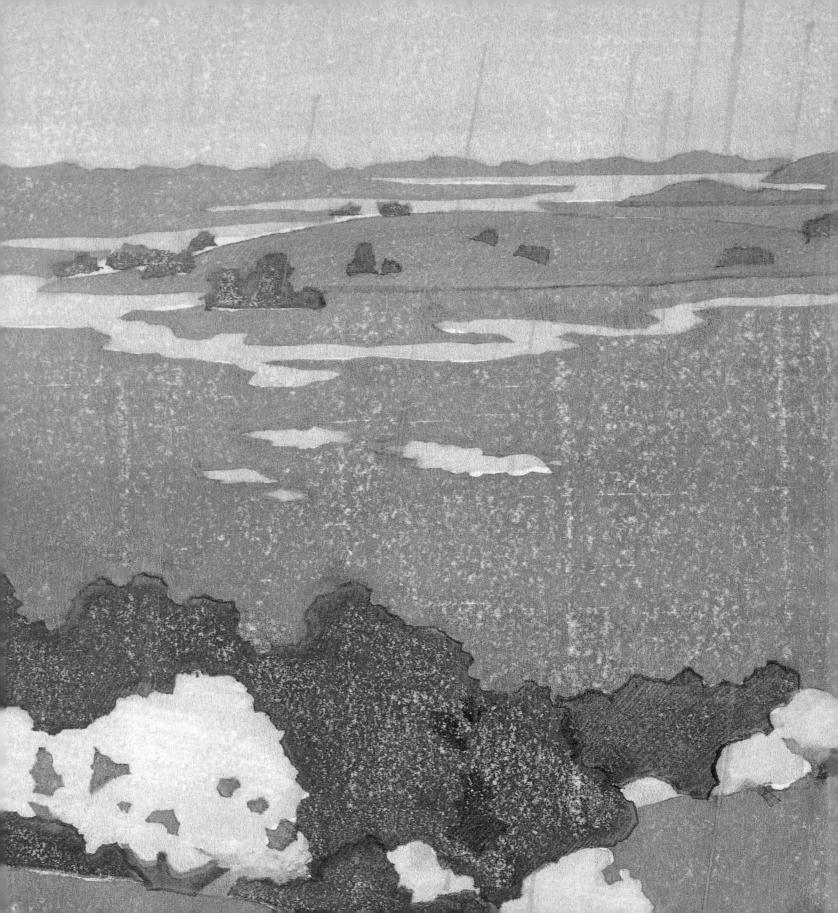

Arthur Wesley Dow

AND AMERICAN ARTS & CRAFTS

Nancy E. Green

AND

Jessie Poesch

THE AMERICAN FEDERATION OF ARTS

in association with

HARRY N. ABRAMS, INC., PUBLISHERS

Harry N. Abrams, Inc.
100 Fifth Avenue
New York, N.Y. 10011
www.abramsbooks.com

Frontispiece: Arthur Wesley Dow, detail of *Rain in May,*
ca. 1909.
Page 54: Augustus Thibaudeau, detail of *Lily Pad in
Reflecting Pond,* ca. 1910.
Page 108: Newcomb Pottery, detail of *Vase* (china-ball
tree design), ca. 1908.

Library of Congress Cataloging-in-Publication Data
Green, Nancy E.
  Arthur Wesley Dow and American arts & crafts /
Nancy E. Green : essays by Nancy E. Green and
Jessie Poesch.
     p.   cm.
  Exhibition itinerary: the Iris and B. Gerald Cantor
Center for Visual Arts, Stanford University, Stan-
ford, Calif., July 13–Sept. 19, 1999, and others.
  Includes bibliographical references.
  ISBN 1-885444-09-5
  ISBN 0-8109-4217-8 (Abrams)
  1. Dow, Arthur W. (Arthur Wesley), 1857–1922—
Exhibitions.   2. Arts and crafts movement—United
States—Exhibitions.   I. Poesch, Jessie J.   II. Iris &
B. Gerald Cantor Center for Visual Arts at Stanford
University.   III. Title.
N6537.D64A4 1999
709'.2—dc21   98-54420
                                                          CIP

Contents

LENDERS TO THE EXHIBITION

Albright-Knox Art Gallery, Buffalo, New York

Amon Carter Museum, Fort Worth, Texas

The Art Museum, Princeton University

Benjamans Art Gallery, Buffalo, New York

Buffalo and Erie County Historical Society

Cathers & Dembrosky, New York

Cambridge City Public Library

Castellani Art Museum, Niagara University, Niagara, New York

The Rare Book and Manuscript Library of Columbia University

Crocker Art Museum

George Eastman House, Rochester, New York

Everson Museum of Art

Fine Arts Museums of San Francisco, Achenbach Foundation for Graphic Arts

Forum Gallery, New York

Gibbes Museum of Art, Charleston

Howard-Tilton Memorial Library, Tulane University, New Orleans

Indianapolis Museum of Art

Herbert F. Johnson Museum of Art, Cornell University

Licking County Historical Society, Newark, Ohio

Los Angeles County Museum of Art

Louisiana State Museum

The Metropolitan Museum of Art

Minneapolis Institute of the Arts

Museum of Art, Rhode Island School of Design

Museum of Fine Arts, Boston

New Orleans Museum of Art

The Newark Museum

H. Sophie Newcomb College, Tulane University

Print Collection, Miriam and Ira D. Wallach Division of Art, Prints, and Photographs, The New York Public Library; Astor, Lenox, and Tilden Foundations

Oakland Museum of California

Gerald Peters Gallery, Santa Fe

Provincetown Art Association & Museum

Richmond Art Museum

San Diego Museum of Art

Strong Museum, Rochester, New York

David Cathers

Theodore B. Donson and Marvel M. Griepp

Peter Falk

Leslie and Joanna Garfield

Stephen Gray

James D. Kaufman

Andrew Terry Keats

Private collection, courtesy Janet Lehr Inc.

Alexandra Sheldon

Mark and Jill Willcox, courtesy Robert Edwards

George and Barbara Wright

Jean and Jim Young

ACKNOWLEDGMENTS

This exhibition examines and celebrates the tremendous influence of one man, Arthur Wesley Dow, on generations of artists, photographers, designers, ceramists, and furniture makers who were part of the American arts and crafts movement. It has been a pleasure working with guest curator Nancy E. Green, chief curator at the Herbert F. Johnson Museum of Art, who brought a high level of knowledge and expertise to the exhibition and catalogue, and contributing author Jessie Poesch, professor emerita, history of art, Tulane University.

At the AFA, the exhibition and accompanying catalogue are, as usual, the result of the collaboration of the entire staff. The efforts of the following staff members, however, deserve special recognition: Klaus Ottmann, curator of exhibitions, and his assistant, Robin Kaye Goodman, for overseeing the organization of the exhibition; Michaelyn Mitchell, head of publications, and her assistant, Tasha Eichenseher, for overseeing the publication of the catalogue; Karen Convertino, registrar, for coordinating the logistics of traveling the exhibition; and Katey Brown, head of education, and Brian Boucher, assistant curator of education, for developing the educational materials. I also want to acknowledge Thomas Padon, director of exhibitions, for his oversight throughout the development of the project.

Thanks also to Brian Wallis, for his skillful editing of the texts, and Susan E. Kelly and Ed Marquand at Marquand Books, for their handsome design.

The many private and institutional lenders, without whose generosity the exhibition could not have come to fruition, are acknowledged with deep gratitude.

We also want to recognize the museums with which we have had the pleasure of working on the national tour of the exhibition: the Iris and B. Gerald Cantor Center for Visual Arts at Stanford University; the Terra Museum of American Art, Chicago; and the Blanden Memorial Art Museum, Fort Dodge, Iowa.

Lastly, we wish to acknowledge the loyal support of the National Patrons of the AFA, as well as the Lila Wallace–Reader's Digest Fund, which supported the project through the AFA's ART ACCESS II initiative.

SERENA RATTAZZI
Director
The American Federation of Arts

ACKNOWLEDGMENTS

An exhibition of this scope can be truly daunting without the help of many people. Friends and colleagues provided invaluable help and suggestions, pointing the way to new information and discussing all sorts of ideas in detail. I would like to thank everyone who has had a part in it. In particular, I would like to thank all these individuals who helped me in my research: David Acton, Worcester Art Museum; Janice Capecci, Oakland Museum; Janice Coco, University of California, Davis; Lorna Condon, Society for the Preservation of New England Antiquities; Maureen Donnelly, Louisiana State Museum; Robert Edwards; Ilene Susan Fort, Los Angeles County Museum of Art; Stephanie Gaskins and James Kyprianos, Ipswich Historical Society; Anne Havinga, Museum of Fine Arts, Boston; James D. Kaufman, Dedham Historical Society; Patricia Keats, California State Historical Society; John Keefe, New Orleans Museum of Art; Martin F. Krause, Jr. and Barry L. Shifman, Indianapolis Museum of Art; Betty Krulik, Spanierman Gallery; Janet Lehr; Nancy Corwin and Sally Main, Newcomb Art Gallery; Susan Montgomery; Marsha Morton, Pratt Institute; Joann Moser, National Museum of American Art; Barbara McCandless, Amon Carter Museum; Nancy Finlay, New York Public Library;

Thomas Piché, Jr., Everson Museum of Art; Becky Simmons, George Eastman House; and Patience Young, the Iris and B. Gerald Cantor Center for Visual Arts at Stanford University.

The staffs of many other institutions were also generous with their time. I would like to thank the Richmond Art Association, the Indiana Historical Society, the Cambridge City Library, the Woodstock Guild, and the Woodstock Public Library for their assistance. Judith Throm and her staff at the Archives of American Art were also very helpful.

For those who shared family collections and personal reminiscences with me, I am greatly indebted. Over the years I have come to rely on the kindness and generosity of Barbara and George Wright and Barbara's brother, Frank Dowd, who sadly passed away last October, for their help with Dow's papers. Jean and Jim Young welcomed me into the world of the Woodstock art community, and Phyllis Munsey provided a wealth of information on her grandfather, Pedro de Lemos. Phyllis and Jerry Mattheis, who now live in the historic Overbeck house, were enthusiastic about my research and provided me with a unique chance to experience their home.

Lastly, I want to express my most sincere gratitude to Stephen Gray, who conceived the idea for this exhibition and who has been generous and helpful at every step of the way; to Jessie Poesch, who has been a fascinating collaborator and a great source of information; and to the staff of the American Federation of Arts—especially Klaus Ottmann, curator of exhibitions; Michaelyn Mitchell, head of publications; Tasha Eichenseher, publications assistant; and Robin Kaye Goodman, exhibitions assistant—for their kindness and patience throughout the entire project.

NANCY E. GREEN

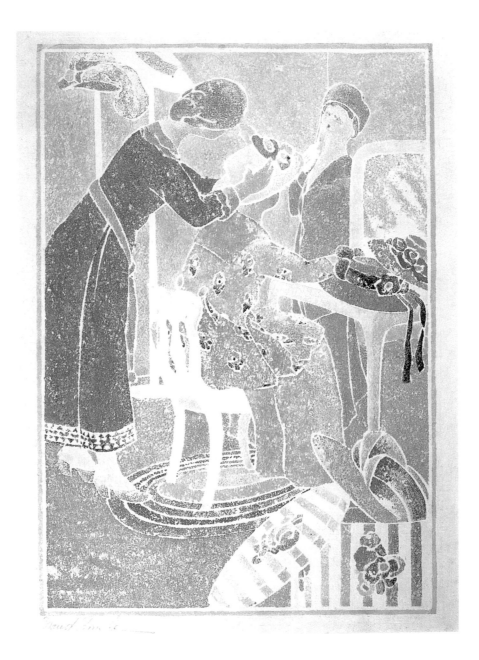

MAUD AINSLIE
The Hat Shop, 1920

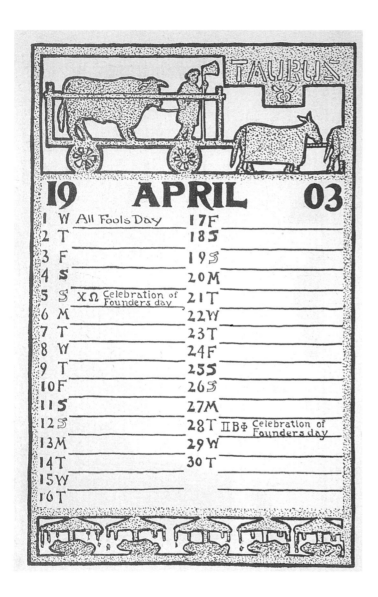

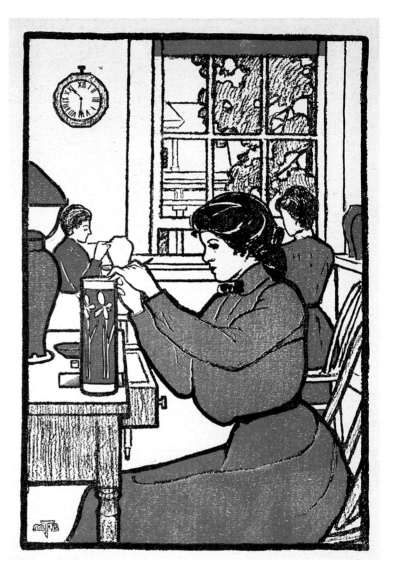

MARY FRANCES BAKER
April, from *Calendar,* 1903

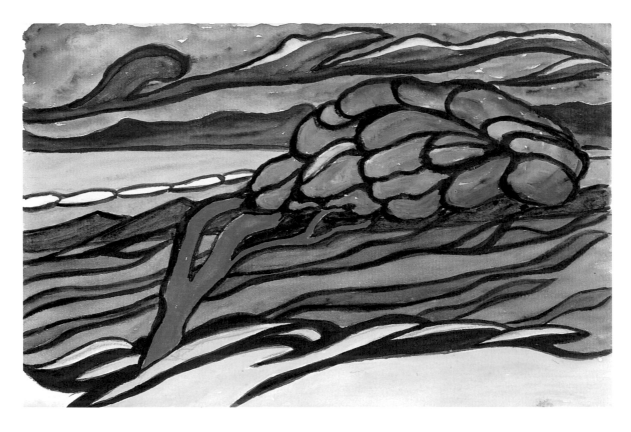

ALVIN LANGDON COBURN
Untitled (water and windblown tree), ca. 1915

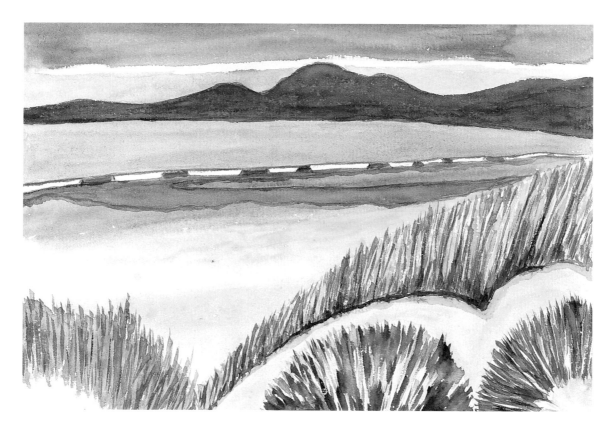

ALVIN LANGDON COBURN
Untitled (landscape with mountain and dune), ca. 1915

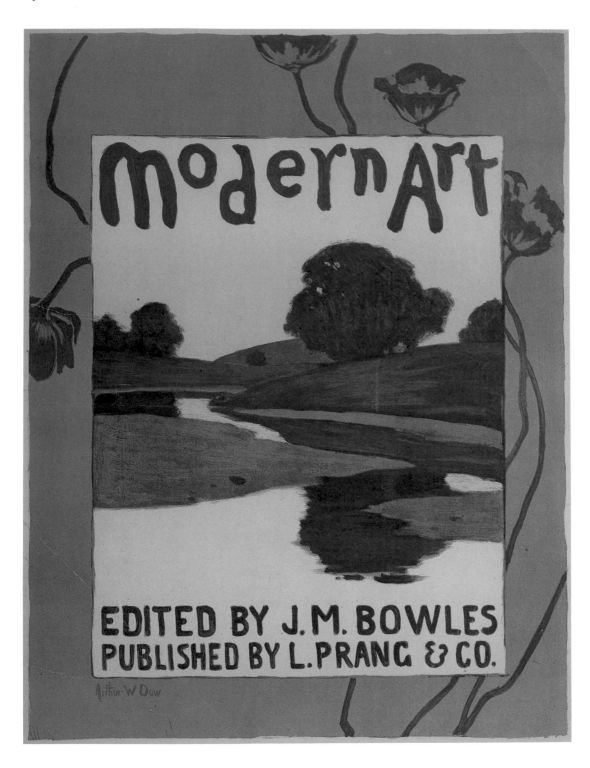

ARTHUR WESLEY DOW
Modern Art, 1895

ARTHUR WESLEY DOW
Bend in a River, ca. 1895

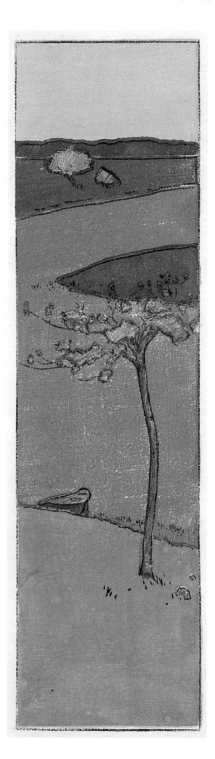

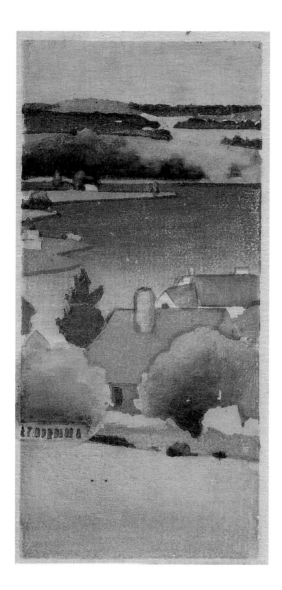

ARTHUR WESLEY DOW
A Bend in the River, ca. 1895

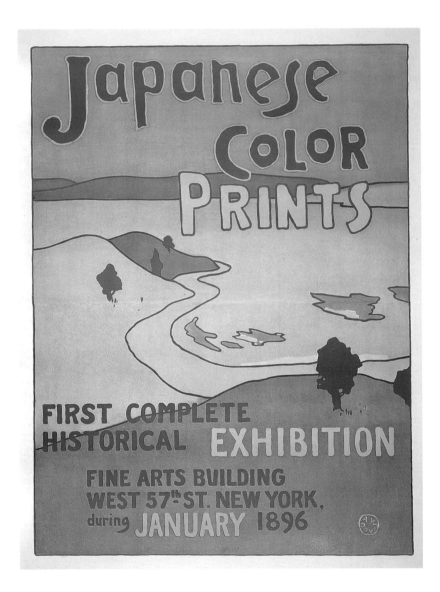

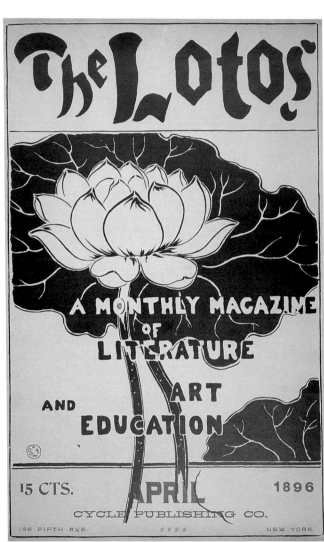

ARTHUR WESLEY DOW
Japanese Color Prints, 1896

ARTHUR WESLEY DOW
The Lotos, 1896

ARTHUR WESLEY DOW
August Moon, ca. 1905

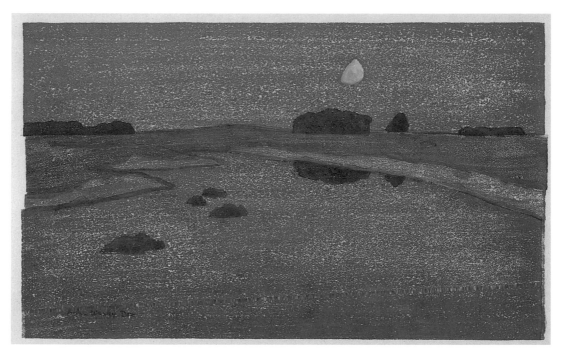

ARTHUR WESLEY DOW
Marsh Creek, ca. 1905

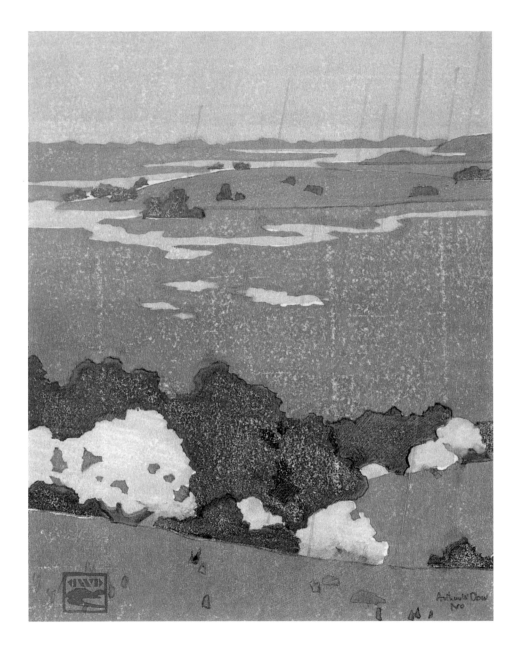

ARTHUR WESLEY DOW
Rain in May, ca. 1907

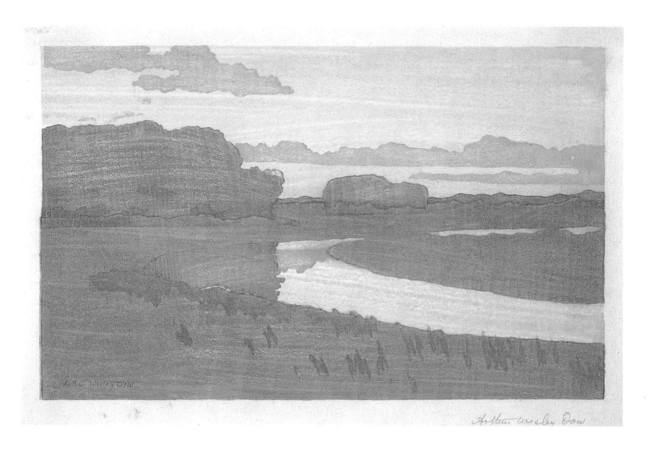

ARTHUR WESLEY DOW
Bend of a River (Sunset), ca. 1908

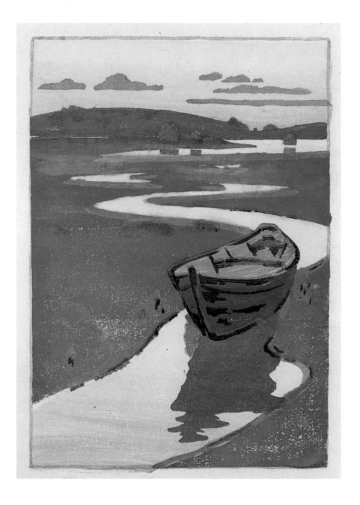

ARTHUR WESLEY DOW
The Derelict (The Lost Boat), 1916

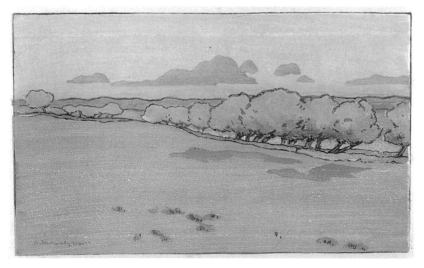

ARTHUR WESLEY DOW
Willows in Bloom, n.d.

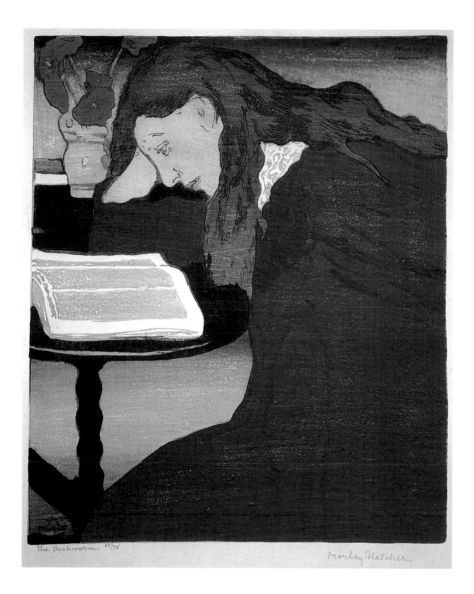

The Bookworm. 33/75   Morley Fletcher.

FRANK MORLEY FLETCHER
The Bookworm, ca. 1920–25

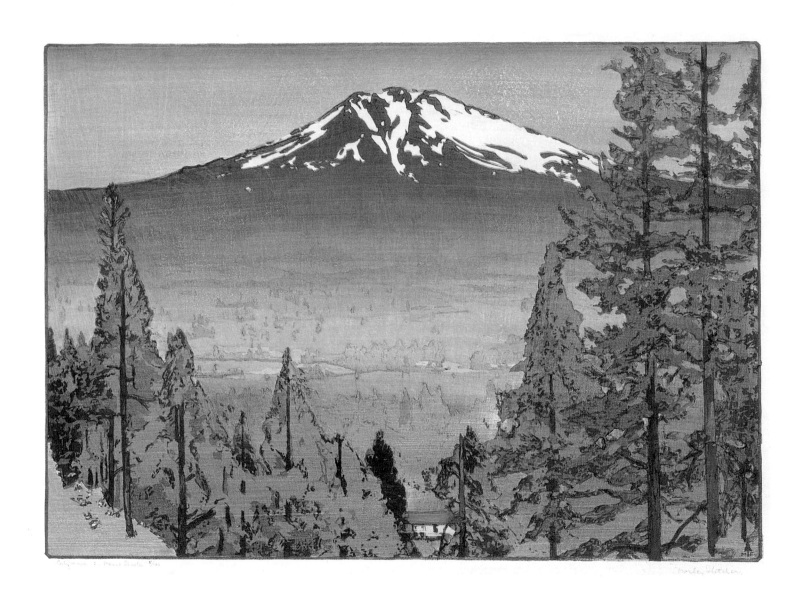

FRANK MORLEY FLETCHER
California. 2. Mount Shasta, ca. 1930

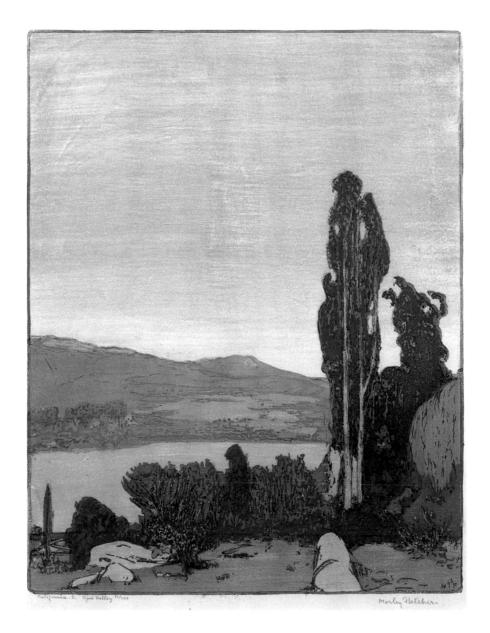

FRANK MORLEY FLETCHER
California. 3. Ojai Valley, ca. 1935

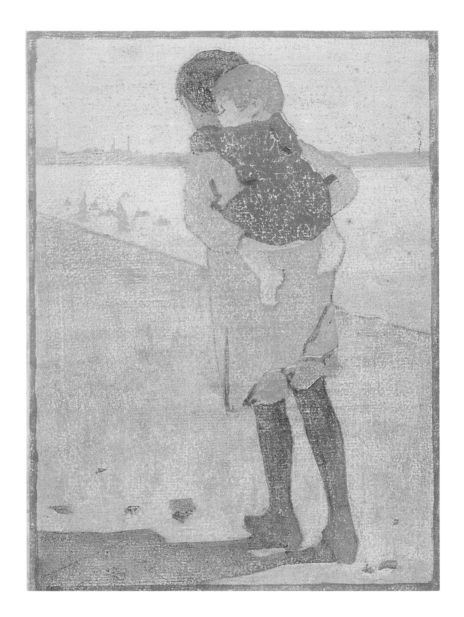

ELIZA DRAPER GARDINER
Pick-A-Back, ca. 1919

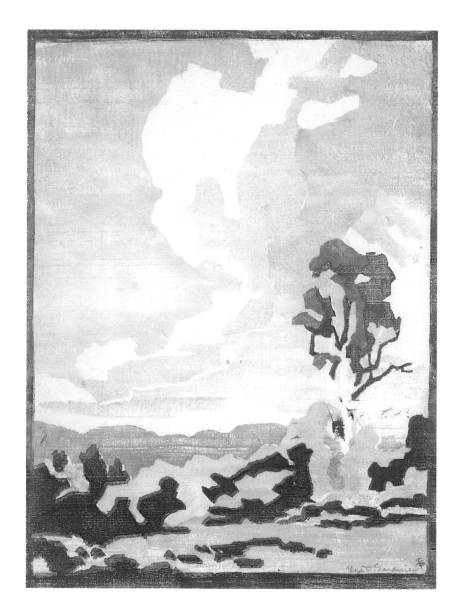

ELIZA DRAPER GARDINER
Passconaway, ca. 1919

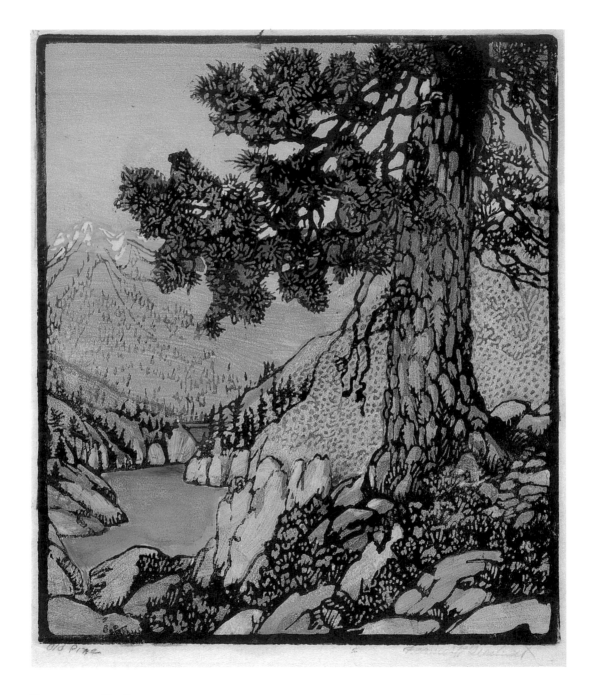

FRANCES H. GEARHART
Old Pine, ca. 1922

FRANCES H. GEARHART
High Blues, n.d.

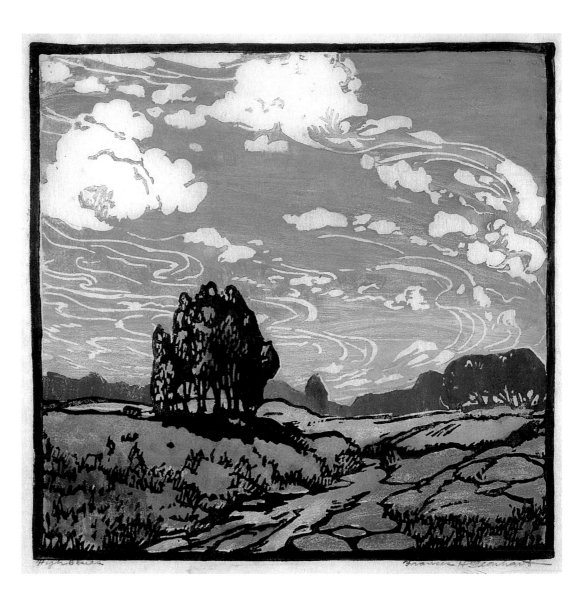

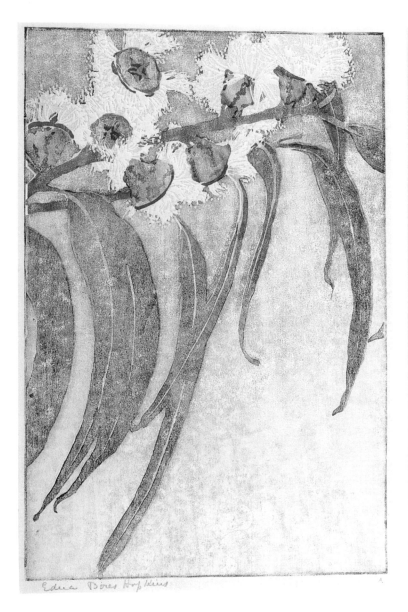

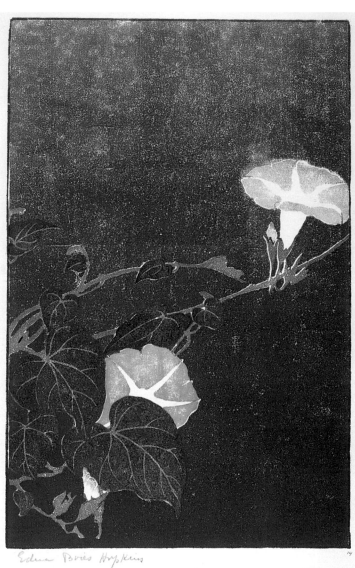

EDNA BEL BOIES HOPKINS
Eucalyptus, ca. 1910

EDNA BEL BOIES HOPKINS
Morning Glory, ca. 1915

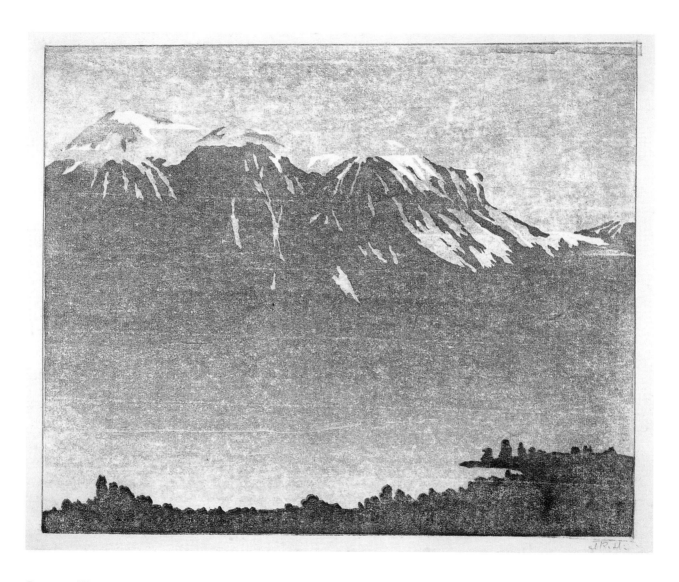

JAMES HOPKINS
Untitled (mountain scene), ca. 1915

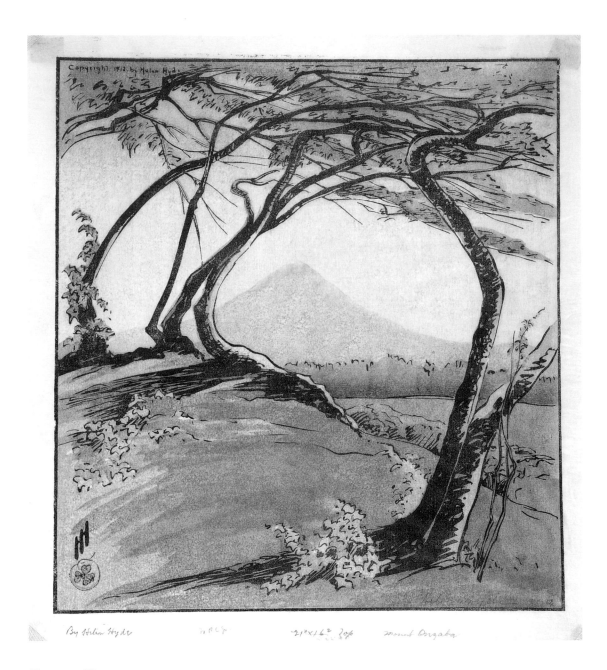

HELEN HYDE
Mount Orizaba, 1912

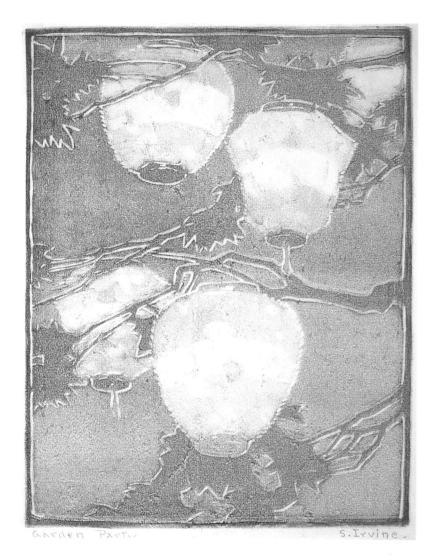

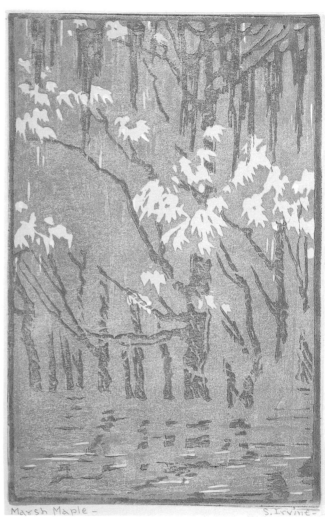

SADIE IRVINE
Garden Party, ca. 1930

SADIE IRVINE
Marsh Maple, ca. 1930

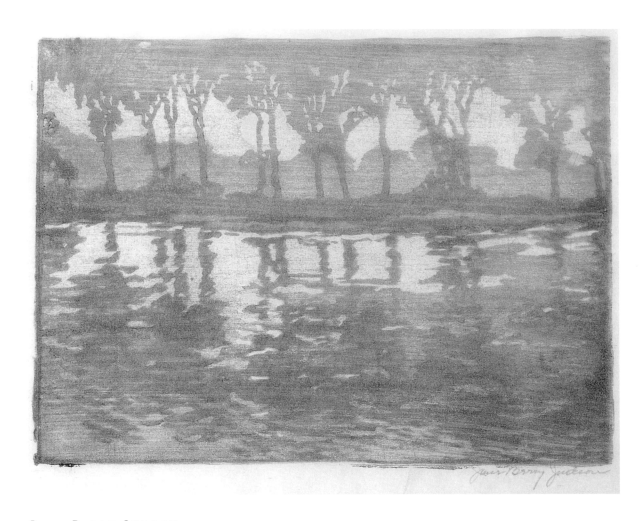

JANE BERRY JUDSON
A Bit of the Forest of Fontainebleau, 1910s

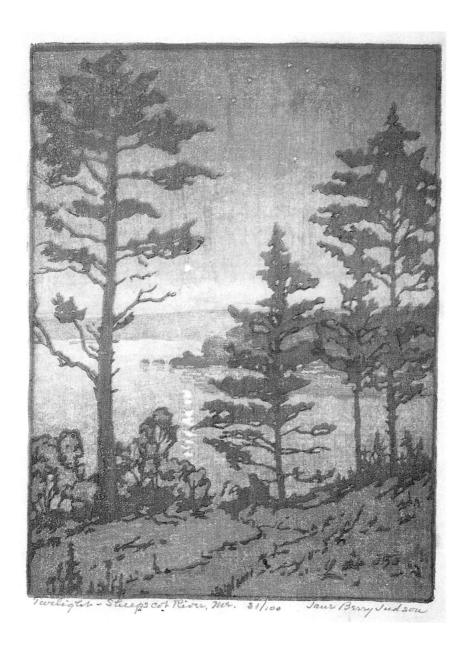

JANE BERRY JUDSON
Twilight: Sheepscot River, Maine, 1910s

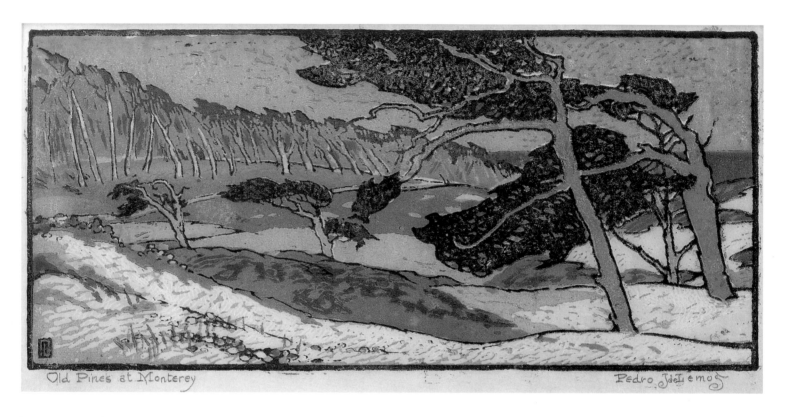

Old Pines at Monterey

Pedro Jde Lemos

PEDRO DE LEMOS
Old Pines at Monterey, ca. 1915

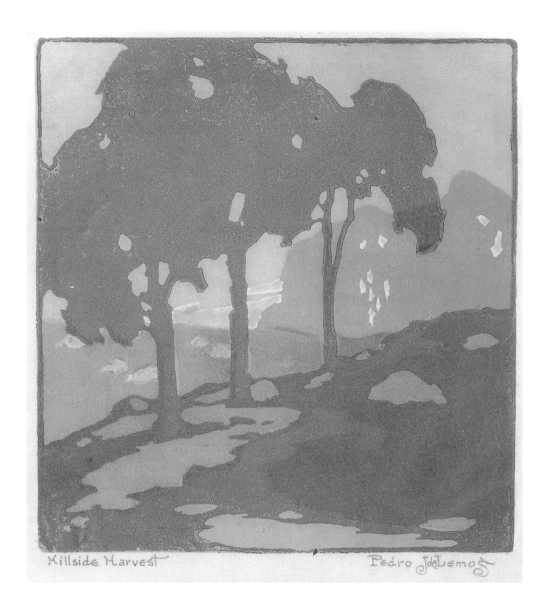

PEDRO DE LEMOS
Hillside Harvest, ca. 1920

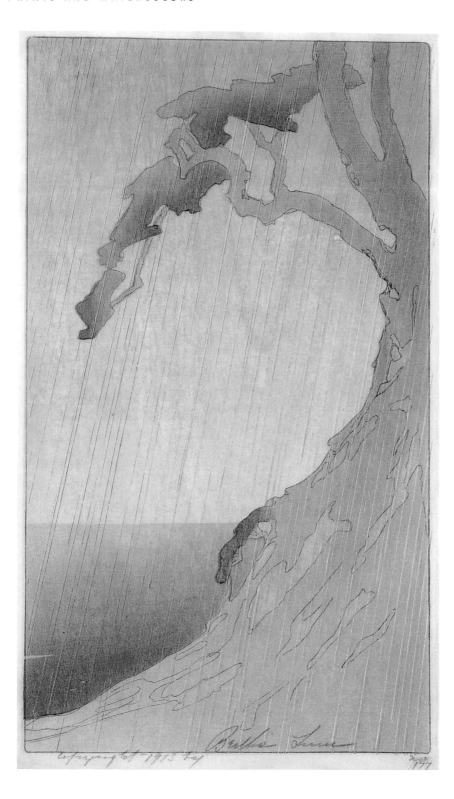

BROR NORDFELDT
The Skyrocket, 1906

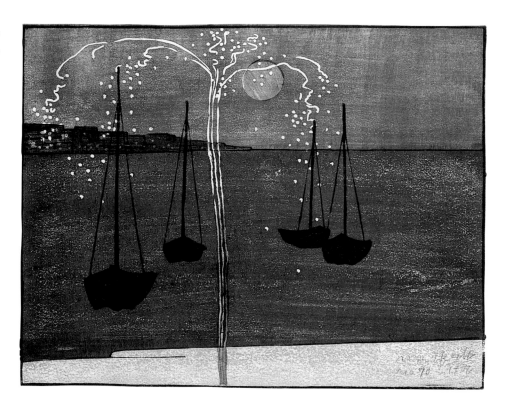

BROR NORDFELDT
Pussy Willows, 1906

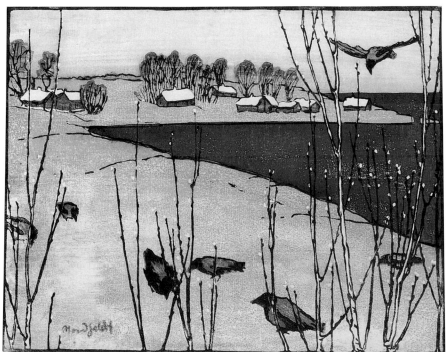

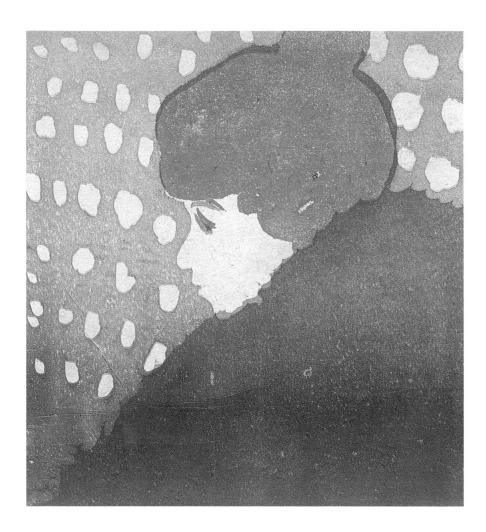

GEORGIA O'KEEFFE
Lady with Red Hair, ca. 1914–16

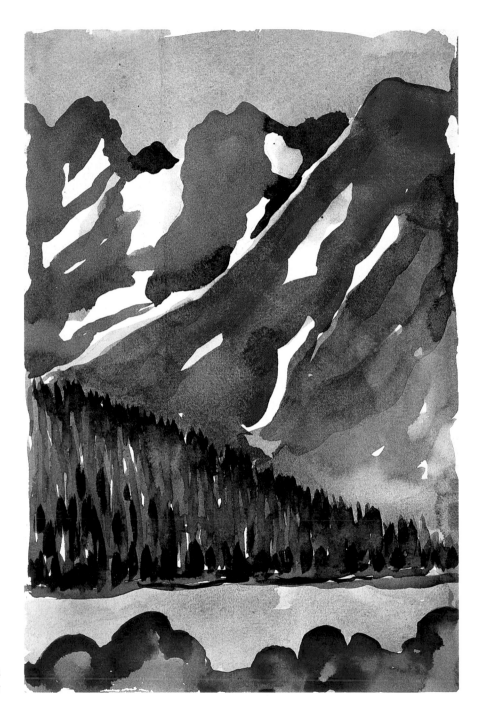

GEORGIA O'KEEFFE
Red and Blue Mountains, ca. 1917

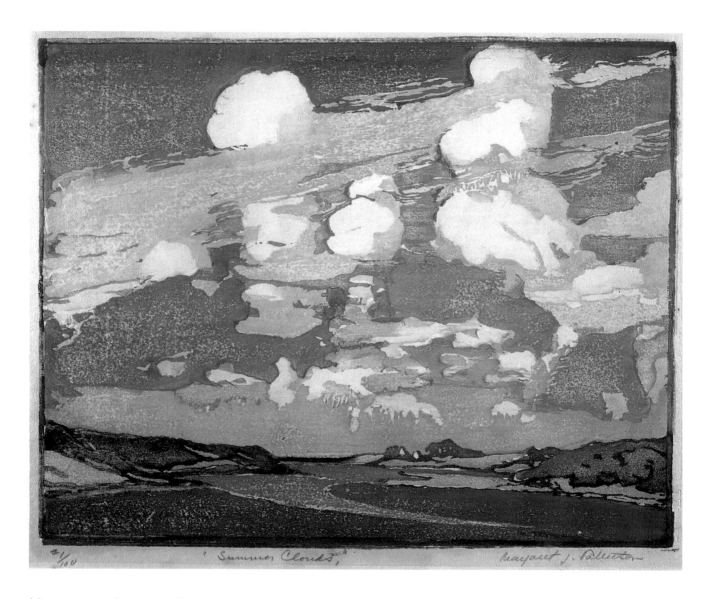

MARGARET JORDAN PATTERSON
Summer Clouds, ca. 1918

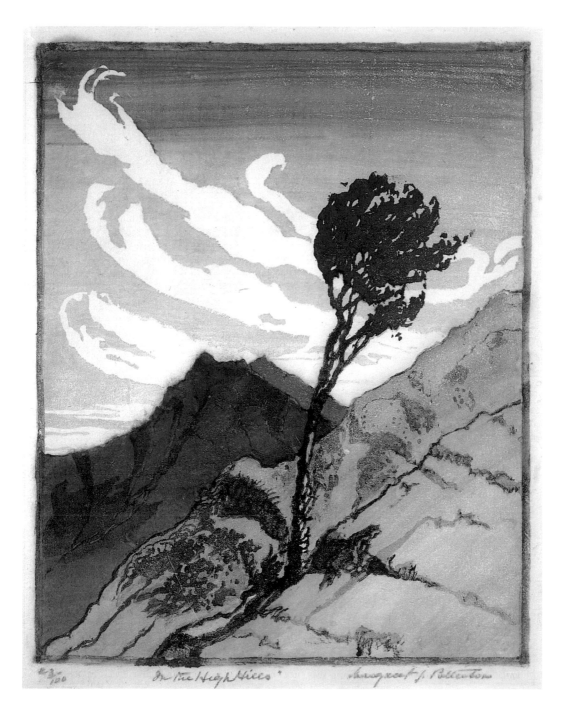

MARGARET JORDAN PATTERSON
In the High Hills, ca. 1925

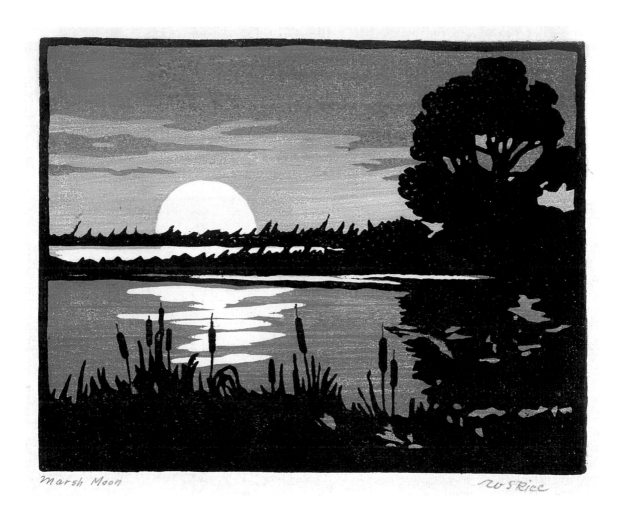

WILLIAM S. RICE
Marsh Moon, ca. 1925

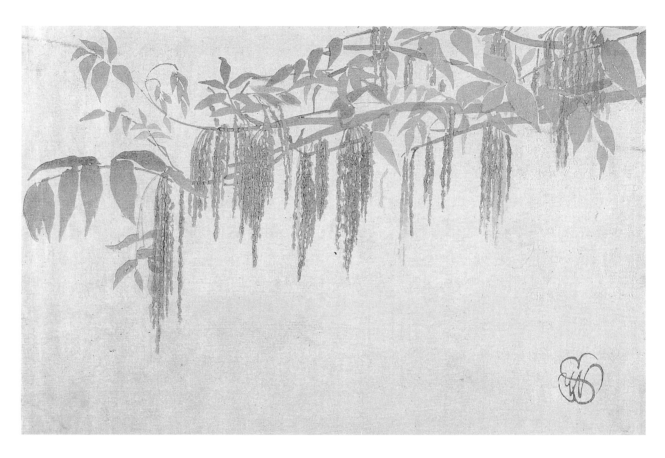

WILHELMINA SEEGMILLER
Flower Study, ca. 1908

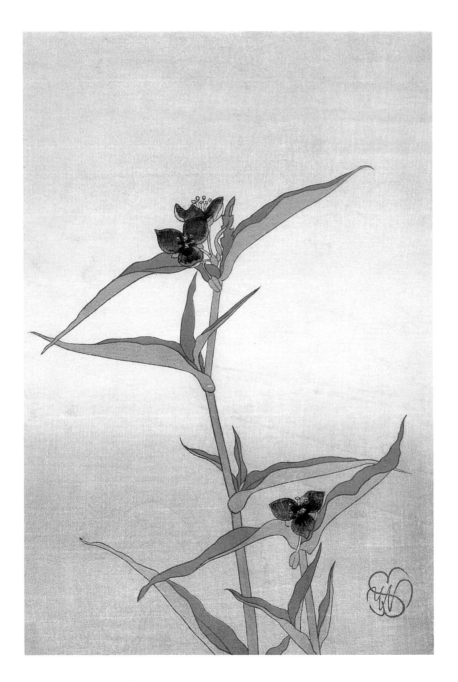

WILHELMINA SEEGMILLER
Flower Study, ca. 1908

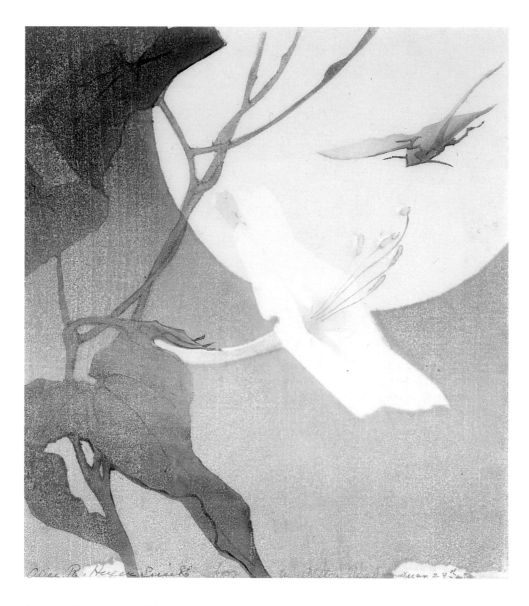

ALICE RAVENEL HUGER SMITH
Moon Flower and Hawk Moth, 1918

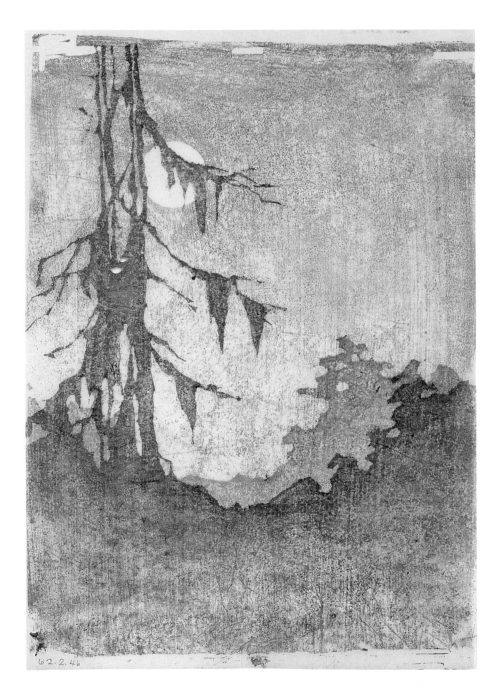

62.2.46

ALICE RAVENEL HUGER SMITH
Untitled (trees with moss and moon), n.d.

ZULMA STEELE ▶
Sheet of Plant Studies and Border Designs, ca. 1910

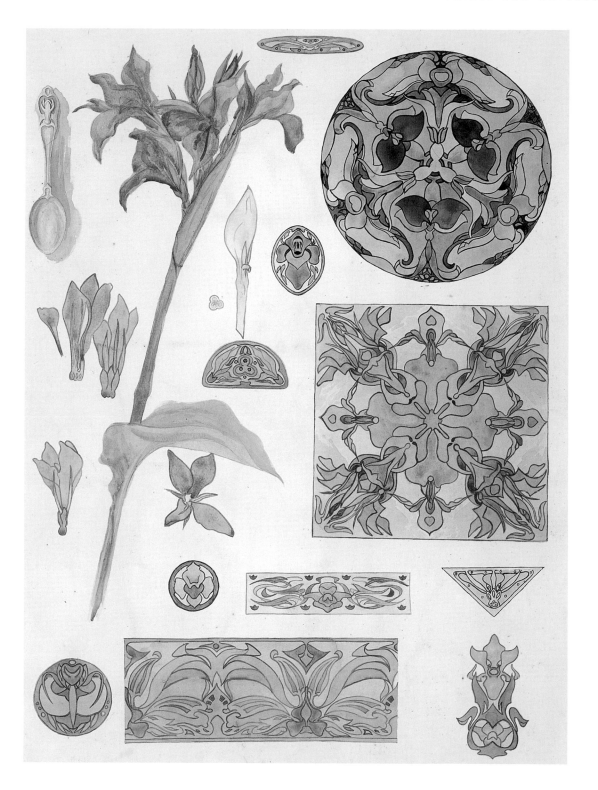

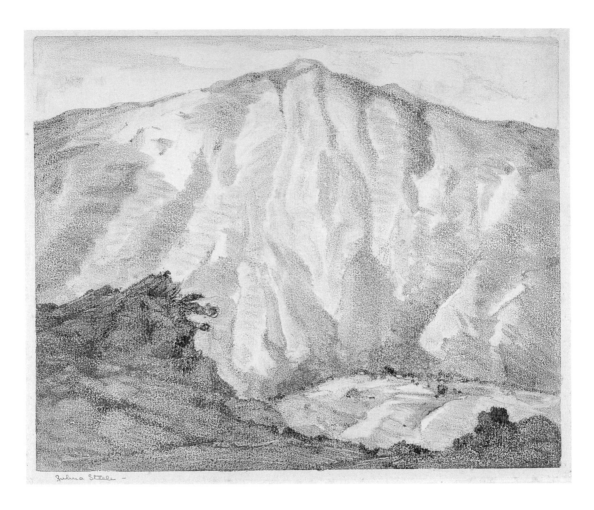

ZULMA STEELE
The High Mountain, ca. 1910–14

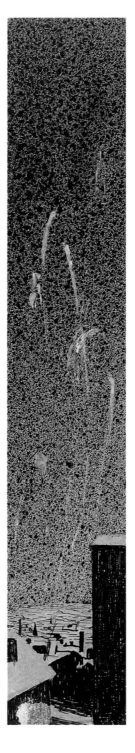
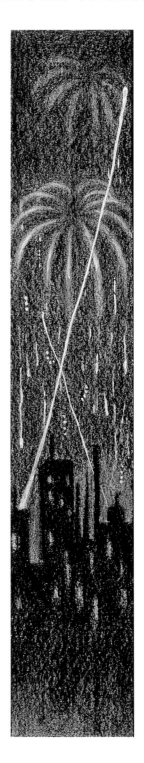

ZULMA STEELE
Fourth of July, ca. 1920

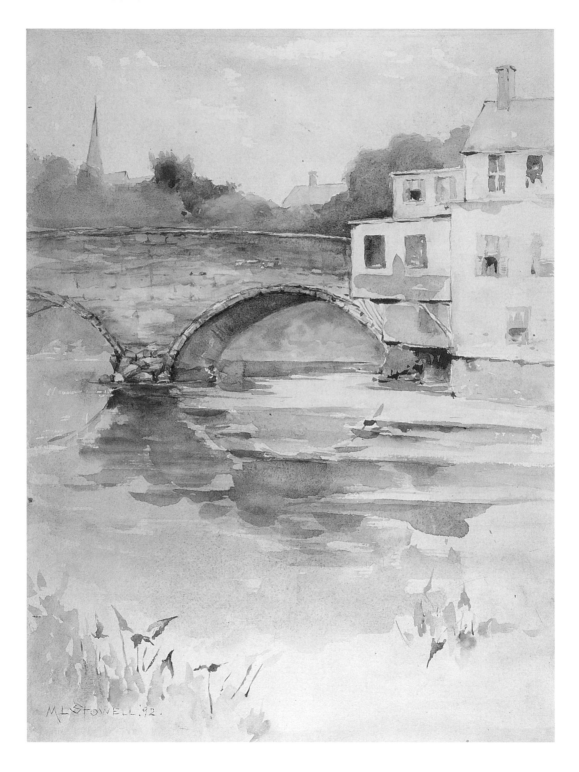

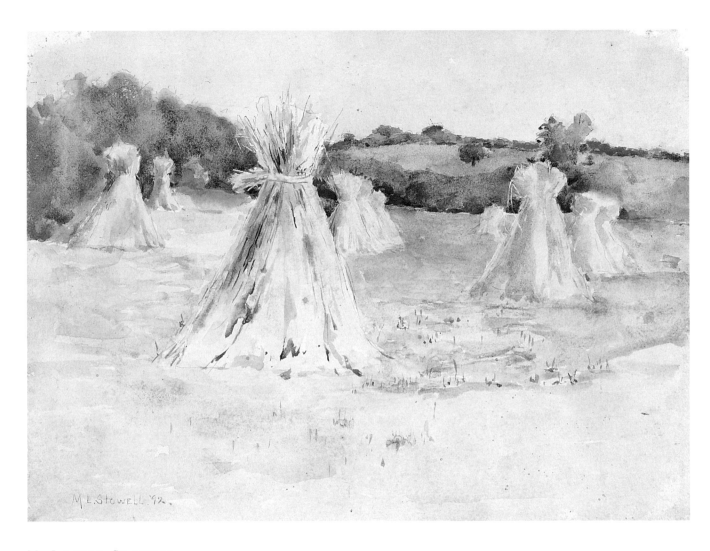

M. LOUISE STOWELL
Untitled (summer landscape), 1892

◄ M. LOUISE STOWELL
Untitled (Ipswich Bridge), 1892

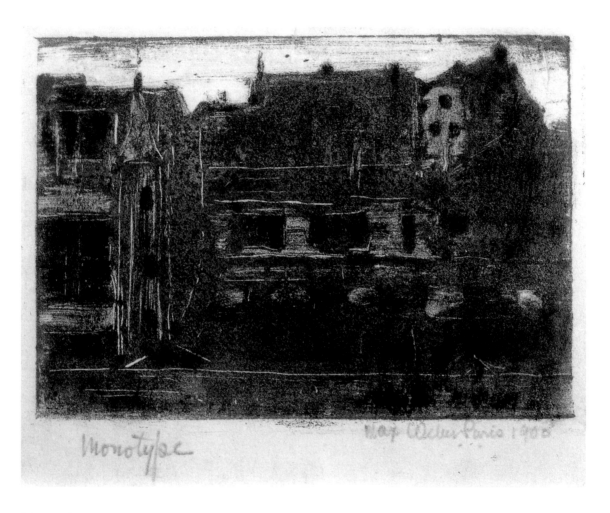

MAX WEBER
Paris Rooftops (Cityscape), 1906

MAX WEBER
Woman Seated at a Table, ca. 1920

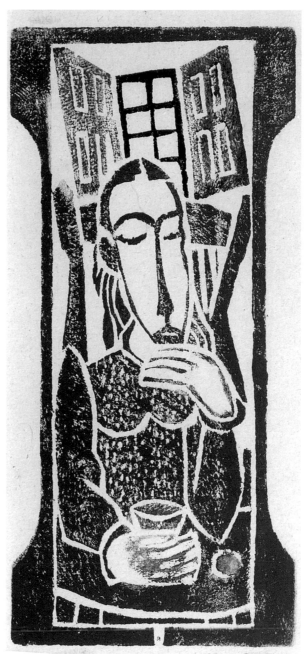

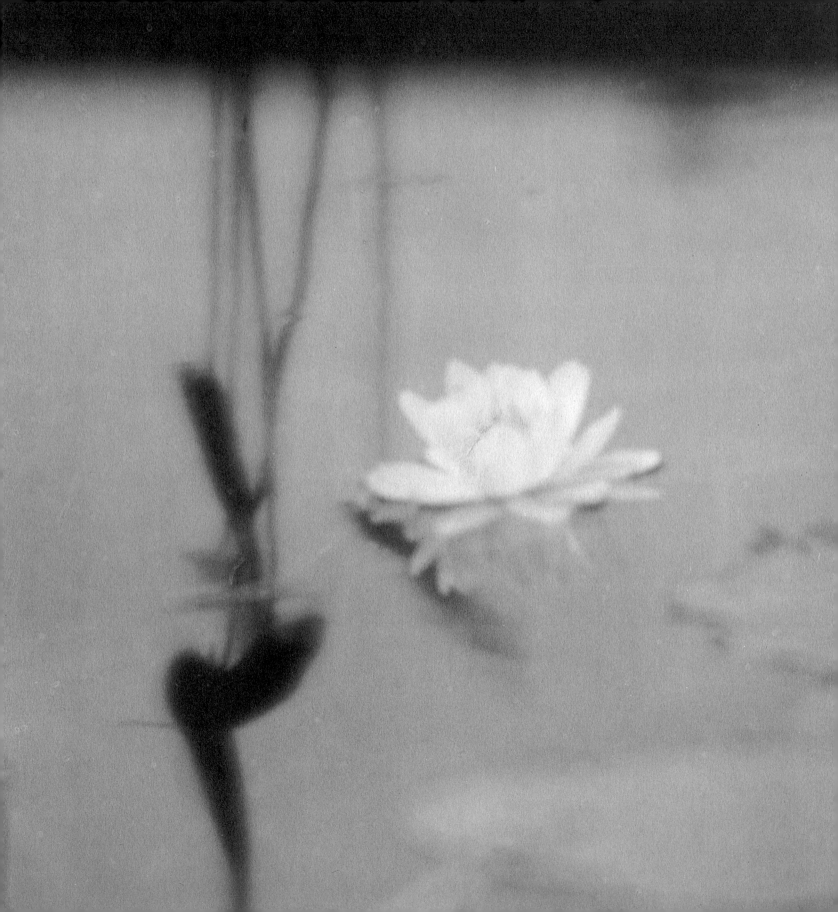

ARTHUR WESLEY DOW,
ARTIST AND EDUCATOR

Nancy E. Green

Probably no artist epitomizes the changes taking place in American art at the turn of the nineteenth century better than Arthur Wesley Dow. Though hardly a household name even in his own day, Dow had a tremendous influence as an artist, teacher, and writer. Trained as a tonalist, Dow gradually assimilated into his work the influences of Japonisme, synthesism, and impressionism (although this was a term he loathed as he associated it with shoddy workmanship). Over his thirty years of teaching, at the Pratt Institute, Teachers College Columbia University, the Art Students League, and his own Ipswich Summer School of Art, Dow integrated all mediums, teaching pottery, design, photography, painting, and printmaking with the same intensity. His tenet, like that of his British arts and crafts counterparts, was to create objects that were well made, finely crafted, and beautifully rendered.

Workshops, art colonies, and art classes emphasizing these ideals proliferated throughout the United States at the end of the nineteenth century. These programs stressed the fine quality of the hand-wrought object and offered classes in every medium with equal emphasis. Dow championed the arts and crafts aesthetic and never considered crafts inferior to fine arts. He taught his students to appreciate the elegance of pure

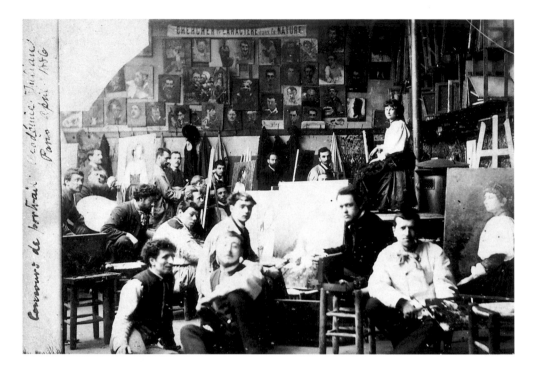

Dow (fourth from right) at the Académie Julian, Paris, 1886. Collection George and Barbara Wright

design (based in nature but not replicating it), placing precedence on no particular technique over any other, as long as the final result was beautiful.

Men as disparate as British playwright Oscar Wilde and midwestern architect Frank Lloyd Wright took up this mission. During his American tour in 1882, Wilde spoke eloquently of the need for an aesthetic of the highest quality in all things: "Let the pitcher by the well be beautiful and surely the labour of the day will be lightened: let the wood be made receptive of some lovely form, some gracious design, and there will come no longer discontent but joy to the toiler." He also stressed that "the mark of all good art is not that the thing is done exactly or finely, for machinery can do as much, but that it is worked

out with the head and the workman's heart."[1] Nearly twenty years later, Wright concurred: "Simplicity in art, rightly understood, is a synthetic, positive quality, in which we may see evidence of mind, breadth of scheme, wealth of detail, and withal, the sense of completeness found in a tree or a flower."[2] But Wright saw the machine as a way to abet a much-desired proliferation of the finely wrought. He said, "In time, I hope to prove that the machine is capable of carrying to fruition high ideals in art—higher than the world has yet seen!"[3]

Like Wilde, Dow preferred the handmade, but, like Wright, he also acknowledged that a machine could create a beautiful object if the operator understood harmonies of color, tone, and form. For Dow, establishing beauty in art was nearly a spiritual calling: it provided shape and meaning to his life. "Art is the most *useful* thing in the world, and the most valued thing," he wrote. "The most useful is always that which is made as finely as possible and completely adapted to its purpose; the most valued because it is the expression of the highest form of human energy, the creative power which is nearest to the divine."[4] These twin debates—the handmade versus the machine-made and decorative art versus fine art— were central to the nineteenth-century arts and craft movement, but they also raged well into the twentieth century and greatly affected the course of modernism in America.

Dow's own approach to the arts and crafts aesthetic came as much from his appreciation of the decorative arts of non-Western cultures, particularly Japan and China, as from his close adherence to the tenets of the English artist and socialist William Morris. The antiquarian interests Dow had as a young man led him to study Early American crafts such as basketmaking, tinwork, and embroidery, all of which he subsequently taught to his students. Later, as a student in Paris, Dow studied the tapestries, porcelains, and carvings at the Musée de Cluny; visited the great African collections at the Trocadero; and took night courses at the Ecole Nationale des Arts Decoratifs, where the critic Francis D. Millet oversaw the students' work. Dow's artistic interests were always far-ranging and eclectic, though the art of the East was ultimately the source for the essential principles of his teaching.

With a clear insistence on the basic principles, Dow made his design program easy to follow. His goal was to give students simple compositional techniques to create beautiful objects. He was an inspired teacher, and students flocked to study with him during his tenures at Pratt Institute (1895–1903), Teachers College Columbia University (1904–1922), the Art Students League (1898–1903), and his summer school in Ipswich, Massachusetts (1891–1907). Painters Georgia O'Keeffe and Max Weber both studied with him and acknowledged his influence. Ceramists Adelaide Alsop Robineau and Marshal Fry took private lessons with him in New York; pottery designers from Newcomb Pottery in New Orleans, including Henrietta Bailey, Marie Levering Benson, Harriet Joor, Roberta Kennon, Desiree and Amelie Roman, and Mary Given Sheerer won scholarships to his summer classes at Ipswich; and two of the Overbeck sisters, Margaret and Mary Frances, studied with him at Columbia. Dow also had a strong influence on developments in photography: Gertrude Käsebier and Alvin Langdon Coburn learned design principles with him, F. Holland Day published Dow's early articles in the arts and crafts journal *Knight Errant* as early as 1893, and young Clarence H. White was hired by Dow to teach a course in photography at Columbia.

Dow was friend and colleague to many of the leading artists, collectors, and scholars of his day, including artists Herman Dudley Murphy, Frank Benson, and Maurice Prendergast; critic/art historian Sadakichi Hartmann; collector Charles Freer; the orientalists William Sturgis Bigelow, Ernest Fenollosa, Edward S. Morse, and Denman Ross; Morse's protégé Bunkio Matsuki, who owned a Japanese art supply store and befriended

Dow in 1892; Sylvester Rosa Koehler, print curator at the Museum of Fine Arts, Boston, who had printed for Prang and advised Dow on process; and ethnologist Frank Hamilton Cushing who stimulated Dow's interest in the American Southwest and in Indian symbols as design.

In 1899 Dow published what was to be the first of twenty editions of his landmark book *Composition: A Series of Exercises in Art Structure for the Use of Students and Teachers* (p. 188). His premise was based on three compositional elements—line, color, and *notan* (a Japanese term that refers to the relation of areas of light and dark)—which could be used to achieve a perfect synthesis through opposition, transition, subordination, repetition, and symmetry. To attain the requisite harmony of these elements (which he had found nowhere in his own art training), Dow sought something "beyond the mere drawing . . . from nature."[5] Many years later, he still strongly rejected the academic approach, reiterating his position in an article for *The Delineator:* "The art lies in the fine choices, not in the truth, likeness to nature, meaning, story-telling or finish. . . . The artist does not teach us to see facts: he teaches us to feel harmonies and to recognize supreme quality."[6]

Dow's *Composition* was compiled from articles originally published in the *Pratt Institute Monthly.* There, Dow discussed in depth the thoughts on aesthetics he had developed with the Asian art scholar Ernest Fenollosa. The book was heavily illustrated with examples of objects from Asian, Aztec, African, Egyptian, Oceanic, pre-Columbian, and Western cultures, thereby encouraging the student to learn—and learn

well—from the decorative principles of design of every culture. "Design" was a word that was then denigrated in academic circles, and by taking up a position in favor of design, Dow drew the lines clearly. He saw composition as the way to forge a discipline in which hand and mind would work together, making aesthetic creativity available to everyone. As a reviewer for the *Boston Transcript* said of *Composition,* "The art student who reads this book carefully and reflects upon what Mr. Dow has put into it will see new light, and will realize that the usual system of education for painters is too automatic and philistine to last."[7]

Word of Dow's teaching methods spread widely, not only through the use of his textbook *Composition* but also through the work of his students, many of whom later became art instructors themselves. As art instruction became a permanent part of kindergarten, elementary, and high-school education, and more women began looking for careers that would use their artistic skills, students sought out programs such as those at Pratt Institute and Columbia University, which emphasized practical skills in design and the decorative arts as well as teaching qualifications. Dow's lasting contribution was to teach art with an eye to both beauty and utility, not just art for art's sake but rather art for the soul's sake. Dow's converts were many and his methods gave form to American modernist thought.

BEGINNINGS

Dow's artistic ambitions began modestly in his hometown of Ipswich, Massachusetts. Solitary and intelligent as a child, he was a good student, interested in languages and history, particularly the Colonial history of Boston's North Shore. He dreamed of continuing his education at Amherst College, but without sufficient funds, this was impossible. Instead, he sought out the Reverend John P. Cowles, who had recently retired from the Ipswich Female Seminary, to tutor him in Latin, Greek, and mathematics while he simultaneously earned a living as an elementary school teacher in nearby Linebrook Parish. In 1879 Dow met the Reverend Augustine Caldwell, an antiquarian of some prestige, who adopted him as his protégé. Together they produced a journal of local history, the *Ipswich Antiquarian Paper,* which Dow illustrated using various printing techniques.[8] Eager as Dow was, the processes of heliogravure and lithography posed many technical problems for the uninitiated, and his best efforts at printmaking were the wood engravings he made of notable pre-Revolutionary homesteads in the area.

This initial foray into art making led Dow to try his hand at painting. Apparently, however, he was uncomfortable with the human form, and his early work consists mostly of landscapes along with occasional animal sketches. In 1880 Caldwell introduced Dow to the Moses Farmer family, who became his first art patrons. Encouraged by these contacts, Dow began formal art classes in April 1880 with the historical and portrait painter Anna K. Freeland in Worcester. This was followed by an apprenticeship in the Boston studio of the painter James M. Stone. There Dow met the famed artist Frank Duveneck, who remained a friend until his death in 1919, and fellow student Minnie Pearson, who later became Dow's wife.

Stone had studied in both Paris and Munich, and he encouraged his eager pupil to do the same. In 1884, after nearly four years of frugal living while teaching art on the North Shore, Dow finally set sail for Paris. As an older student proficient in French, Dow's experience was quite different from that of most of his fellow students, and he avoided the high jinks and Bohemian posturing that preoccupied many of them. Rather, he restricted himself to moderate entertainments (he did see Sarah Bernhardt perform) and lived a spartan life, hoping to make his savings last. Moreover, he worked hard to please his professors, Gustave Boulanger and Jules Lefèbre. He earnestly sought their praise and, like most of his fellow students, aimed for a favorable hanging of his work by the Salon jurists. Arthur Johnson, Dow's earliest biographer, described this period as "a season of experimentation, a season of trial and error and out of it came the conviction that sunsets and twilights, soft coloured landscapes were the things that spoke to him personally the most poetic language of art. From this decision of his first year in Paris he swerved very little throughout all his creative years."[9]

Gradually, however, Dow wearied of the academic system with its archaic rules and acceptance of mediocrity. In 1886, with his friend and fellow art student Henry Kenyon, Dow traveled to Pont Aven, an artists' colony on the Breton coast. Kenyon and Dow found the once-quiet fishing village overrun with artists seeking unusual views that might win favor with the Salon committee.

Novel viewpoints were hard to come by, and competition among the students was fierce. In addition, that summer marked the arrival of the radical colorists Paul Gauguin, Paul Serusier, and Emile Bernard. This group was formulating bold new ideas about abstraction and synthesis, and they tended to separate themselves from the academic painters, an attitude that did not sit well with the more conservative American artists like Dow. But, despite his rejection of Gauguin and all he stood for, Dow soon recognized how stale his own academic efforts were. When Gauguin and his followers held an anti-academic protest exhibition at the Café Volpini across the street from the 1889 Exposition Universalle in Paris,

even Dow could hardly ignore the implications for the future of modern art.

Upon his return to Boston in 1889, Dow began in earnest to search out a viable alternative to the frustrations and restrictions of his strict academic training. An avid reader, he spent hours at the Boston Public Library searching through books on Italian *trecento*, Aztec, Oceanic, African, and Egyptian art. Though his imagination was fired by all these studies, Dow's greatest epiphany occurred when he encountered the work of the Japanese *ukiyo-e* printmaker Katsushika Hokusai (1760–1849). In an oft-quoted letter to Minnie, he wrote, "It is now plain to me that Whistler and Pennell whom I have admired as

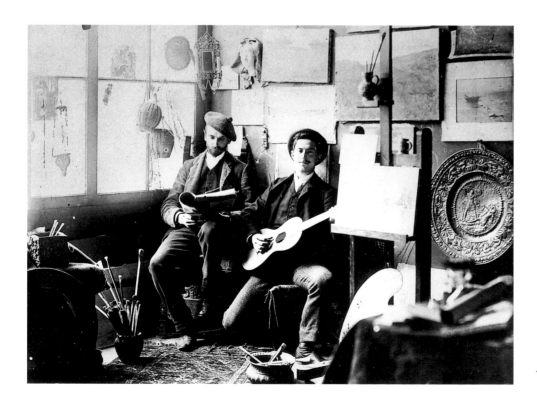

Dow (right) with his friend Henry Kenyon in the studio Dow established in Ipswich soon after their return from Paris, ca. 1890. Collection George and Barbara Wright

great originals are only copying the Japanese. One evening with Hokusai gave me more light on composition and decorative effect than years of study of pictures. I surely ought to compose in an entirely different manner and paint better."[10]

Dow's enthusiasm for Hokusai led him to Boston's Museum of Fine Arts, where the Japanese collection was presided over by the noted scholar Ernest Fenollosa.[11] In his astute analysis of Japanese art, Fenollosa observed that its characteristic spirituality was based on abstraction, simplification, and a harmonious synthesis of forms. Dow's goal was to apply this same aesthetic to Western fine and decorative art, and to make that art available to a wide audience at a reasonable price. Idealistically, Dow considered that the Japanese people, even as young children, possessed an inherent appreciation of good art based on their use of everyday objects of beauty; it was this universal message of beauty that Dow wished to teach. As he later said in a lecture to a group of Boston art students, "Teach the child to know beauty when he sees it, to *create it,* to love it, and when he grows up he will not tolerate the ugly. In the relations of lines to each other he may learn the relation of lives to each other; as he perceives color harmonies, he may also perceive the fitness of things."[12]

"PAINTING WITH BLOCKS"

It is not surprising that the *ukiyo-e* woodcuts of Hokusai inspired Dow in his quest for a universal, democratic art form. This style of Japanese printmaking depicted the pleasures of everyday life—landscapes, actors, geishas, and historical scenes. These "pictures of the floating world" were inexpensive and, therefore, very popular with members of the new Japanese merchant class, who wanted to own art but could not afford the paintings and screens made for the aristocracy. *Ukiyo-e* woodcuts combined skilled craftsmanship in the design and cutting of the blocks with a simple aesthetic based on line and space. Nature was used as a reference point, but the finished product was often highly abstract, depending on the inclination of the individual artist. To Western artists, accustomed to careful modeling and perspective, the *ukiyo-e* aesthetic seemed flat, decorative, and thoroughly modern.

In the early 1890s, Dow was not alone in his enthusiasm for Japanese art. Years earlier, when Dow was in Pont Aven, Gauguin had organized an exhibition of Japanese prints for the students staying at the Pension Gloanec. American artists John LaFarge and James McNeill Whistler, as well as the French impressionists, had also drawn on the aestheticized spirituality of Eastern art. And Sylvester Koehler, the print curator at Boston's Museum of Fine Arts, had embarked on a thorough study of Japanese printmaking processes. In 1892, in an experiment that would become a lifelong passion, Dow first attempted his own *ukiyo-e* style woodcuts. He enthusiastically wrote to Minnie that what he sought in his own work was "not any imitation of the Japanese but their refinement, their brilliant and powerful execution, subtle composition, and all the ennobling influences that come from them."[13]

Meanwhile, in the summer of 1891, Dow had opened the Ipswich Summer School of Art, where he had initiated courses in traditional American crafts such as weaving, ceramics, and candle-making, as well as fine art classes in painting and printmaking.[14] Beginning with only a handful of students, the program grew steadily and by 1903 there were nearly two hundred students in residence. By 1904, however, Dow's time was so encumbered that he relegated much of the teaching to two of his Pratt colleagues, Ralph Johonnot and Grace Cornell.[15] During its sixteen-year run, Dow took only one year off from the summer school—in 1896, when he traveled to Europe to study *trecento* art—and it ran successfully until 1907, when other demands on his time warranted closing it down. It was a popular school, similar to many other arts and crafts programs then available around the country, training students to appreciate decoration and design in all the arts.

An 1892 advertising circular for the school claimed that "the method to be used would be synthetic and would aim at developing a creative grasp in rendering subject rather than a narrow line of abstract technique."[16] In true Ruskinian manner, students were encouraged to use the natural resources of the neighborhood—grasses and barks for baskets, clays and local sands for pots, and the reeds and rushes for weaving— "to convey Nature's great lessons of use and beauty."[17] Photographer Alvin Langdon Coburn, who attended the school in 1902 and 1903, later recalled that it was Dow who had taught him to appreciate the beauty of Japanese art: "I think that all my work has been influenced to a large extent and beneficially by this oriental back-

ground, and I am deeply grateful to Arthur Dow for this early introduction to its mysteries."[18] Other students remembered the magic of these summer months spent in Ipswich, a time when they felt at one with the nature surrounding them and their own efforts to create.[19]

In keeping with the tenets of his teaching, when Dow began to experiment with traditional *ukiyo-e* printmaking he performed all three parts of the process—design, woodblock cutting, and printing—unlike his Japanese counterparts. His first "pillar" prints, using watercolor on soft Japanese tissue, are all essentially the same size, approximately five by two inches. Each image is carefully calculated to achieve the grandest impact within a confined area. In developing his technique, Dow drew on the research of curator Sylvester Koehler. In 1892 Koehler organized an exhibition of Japanese woodcut printmaking at the Smithsonian Institution, in cooperation with the Bureau of Engraving and Printing of the Japanese Ministry of Finance. The exhibition featured a complete set of printmaking tools and materials, donated to the Smithsonian by T. Tokuno, chief of the bureau. The following year, the Smithsonian published Tokuno's article "Japanese Wood-cutting and Wood-cut Printing," edited and annotated by Koehler, which described the *ukiyo-e* printing process in great detail. British artist and educator Frank Morley Fletcher, then teaching at the Central School for Arts and Crafts in London, was greatly influenced by Tokuno's article and immediately began his own experiments in *ukiyo-e* woodcut with the help of his friend and colleague John Batten.[20] Like Dow, Fletcher had studied at the Académie Julian

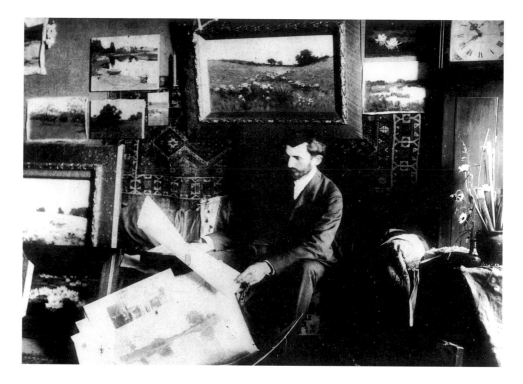

Dow in his Ipswich studio, ca. 1895.
Collection George and Barbara Wright

in Paris in 1888, and his discovery of Japanese art a few years later provided an awakening of inspiration.

By 1895 Dow had completed a number of prints based on *ukiyo-e* works, which he called the *Ipswich Prints,* and Fenollosa mounted a show of them in the Japanese corridor of the Museum of Fine Arts, Boston. Dow later described the purpose of the *Ipswich Prints* this way: "My intention was to make it purely a *picture*-book; not to represent any place, any time of day, or season very realistically, but rather, in an imaginative manner, to use some beautiful groupings of lines and shapes, chosen from the scenery of the old New England town, as a groundwork for different color schemes, a pattern, so to speak, for a mosaic of hues and shades. . . . This possibility of varia-

tion, of search for new color harmonies, the constant surprise from unexpected changes of hue and effect, led me to adopt 'wood-painting' as a means of expression. The origin of the ideas which culminated in these prints can be traced to the observations and fancies of childhood."[21]

Fenollosa's essay for the modest catalogue of the show speaks glowingly of Dow's achievement and emphasizes the woodcut's advantages: "This method of printing utilizes the lost chances, since the block, once carved, saves the repetition of the drawing and allows labor to concentrate on the new color problem."[22] Dow carved his designs for the *Ipswich Prints* from pine (later he switched to the harder maple), using the grain and texture of the wood to reinforce his images. He employed water-color or powdered colors mixed with water and a thin paste or gum or glycerine to fix his tones. Using a Japanese *baren* (made from a bamboo leaf stretched over a hollow pasteboard disk) for rubbing, he produced a variety of results, some muted and gently rendered, some bright with saturated color. Unlike the Japanese, Dow rarely carved a key block to be printed as an overlay at the end, providing detail and outline. Rather, in his case, the colors themselves provide a patterning that serve to layer and flatten the spaces in a thoroughly modernist manner.

For Dow, much of the attraction of this technique was the physical act of creating the woodcut print, beginning with the design and cutting of the blocks. This labor-intensive method of printing reflects the general attitude of the arts and crafts movement, which held that the individual artist should be responsible for the entire production process. From design to cutting the blocks to hand printing each image, often in a myriad of color variations, Dow's method reiterated the strength of his commitment to the craft of creating. And the endless possible variations filled him with pleasure. In *Composition,* he wrote, "The masters of music have shown the infinite possibilities of variation—the same theme appearing again and again with new beauty, different quality and complex arrangement. Even so can lines, masses and colors be wrought into musical harmonies and endlessly varied. The Japanese color print exemplifies this, each copy of the same subject being varied in shade or hue or

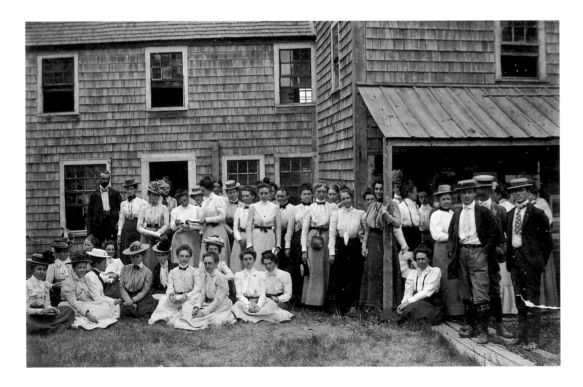

Ipswich Summer School of Art (Dow standing at far left), ca. 1903. Ipswich Historical Society. Photograph Susan Howard Boice.

disposition of masses to suit the restless energy of the author."[23] For Dow, each print was a new exploration, a new experiment, that allowed him to revisit the same themes over and over, each time with a fresh eye. His exhibition of *Ipswich Prints,* though modest in scale and design, included fifteen designs printed in enough color combinations to total two hundred prints.

One artist inspired by this exhibition was a young Rhode Island School of Design student, Eliza Draper Gardiner. Dow's show was probably Gardiner's first exposure to American color woodcuts, and over the course of her long career, she created numerous color woodcuts herself. In her capacity as a teacher at the Moses Brown School in Providence from 1892 to 1908, and later at the Rhode Island School of Design, where she taught from 1908 to 1939, Gardiner employed Dow's design principles. After publication of *Composition* in 1899, she used it as her textbook, ensuring that the next generation of students would carry on her appreciation of Dow's accomplishment.

In 1896 Dow had another show of the *Ipswich Prints,* this time at the Vickery Gallery in San Francisco, and it was probably there that Helen Hyde, who was experimenting with color etching at the time, first encountered his work. Alternatively, the two may have met at the Macbeth Gallery in New York, which represented both of them in the late 1890s and early 1900s. Hyde moved to Japan in 1903, and Dow visited her there that fall. In Japan, he investigated textile and pottery production, visited print dealers, and took printmaking lessons with two of Hyde's instructors, Murata

Shijiro and Kano Tomonobu. In his diaries from the Japan trip, Dow specifically mentions going to Hyde's studio and viewing her work. Her images, mostly figurative and quite different from Dow's, depict Japanese subjects in a sentimental way, but compositionally they relate to his design ideals.[24]

Dow was one of the first Western artists who did not simply imitate Japanese art, but who actually used the traditional Japanese woodcut technique to create modernist prints. He won a medal for his prints from the Boston Mechanics Association and an honorable mention at the Pan-American Exposition in Buffalo in 1901. But more importantly, through his prints Dow achieved his goal of providing quality art at a reasonable price. As critic Peyton Boswell said of Dow's prints, "They occupy a middle ground between the art demands of the wealthy and those of the poor, and satisfy both. . . . Although not costing much, they are real art and fulfill their mission to be decorative and bring happiness."[25]

DOW AS TEACHER

In 1895 Dow and Fenollosa were invited by educator Frederic Pratt to teach a joint course at the newly founded Pratt Institute in Brooklyn. Pratt Institute had opened in 1888, offering an unusual curriculum in fine and decorative arts designed for students from kindergarten through high school, as well as some higher level classes. In September 1895 Dow wrote to Pratt, describing the goal of their proposed course as "the endeavor to give pupils a stimulus to produce strong original work to start them in a line of thought and study which shall enlarge their powers in any field of art which they may choose."[26] Once hired, Dow (without Fenollosa, who had since withdrawn) used the class to emphasize the importance of Japonisme to the decorative arts. As Dow later wrote, the key to his teaching was discovering the student's "personal interpretation or idea of beauty. Not the mere subject, but the way he sees it, interests us most."[27] But at the same time, he did not neglect art teacher training, since that was the role many Pratt students would assume upon graduation. Dow's desire was to provide an appropriate grounding that could be exploited by the individual student to achieve his or her own career goals, and it is impressive how many of his graduates went on to become successful artists, artisans, teachers, and architects.

Many of these artists had long careers as printmakers and teachers and Dow's fame spread. Edna Bel Boies, who had studied art in Cincinnati along with Ethel Mars, Maud Squire, and James Hopkins (whom she married in 1904), came to Pratt Institute in 1899 and experimented with designs for ceramics and lamps, all with an eye to line, *notan,* and color. Her scrapbook, which she kept from November 1902 through April 1903, shows just how greatly Dow influenced her. For instance, she wrote out these Dow-like instructions for wood-block printing: "The most important part of the process is the printing which is done on moist paper with watercolors. The ink or color is applied with a brush, and the printing effected by hand pressure. To this procedure much of the beauty of the result may

be attributed."[28] Boies subsequently imparted this process of color woodcut to her friends, Ethel Mars and Maud Squire, who both went on to become influential Provincetown woodcut artists. (Mars later taught the multiblock method to both Ada Gilmore Chaffee and Margaret Jordan Patterson, another former student of Dow's.[29]) Another Provincetown printmaker influenced by Dow was the Kentucky-born Maud Ainslie, who spent a summer at the Ipswich Summer School of Art before the turn of the century.

Pamela Colman Smith, who had been raised in Jamaica and England, studied with Dow at Pratt Institute in 1896–97. After graduation, she worked as an illustrator, and exhibited at Macbeth Gallery alongside Robert Henri. In 1899 she returned to England with her father and continued her design and illustration career. There Smith became involved with the British avant garde, especially the Celtic Revival group that included William Butler Yeats, Walter Crane, E. Gordon Craig, and Ellen Terry. Her work combined folklore, symbolism, and the occult with strongly synaesthetic musical interpretations, while retaining the unusual perspectives and design of Japanese prints. She did not relinquish her American connections, however, and it was probably through Gertrude Käsebier, whom she knew at Pratt, that she met Alfred Stieglitz. In 1907 Smith became the first nonphotographic artist—and the first woman—to have an exhibition at Stieglitz's gallery 291.[30]

Wilhelmina Seegmiller, an 1899 graduate from Pratt Institute, was director of art instruction in the Indianapolis public schools until her death in 1913. There, she sought to establish technical standards while stimulating creative activity in schoolchildren. She was the author of several textbooks that include illustrations derived from Dow's *Composition,* as well as images of textiles, rugs, pottery, and painting from the world's best museums. With a true arts and crafts mission, her ambition was not only to teach the child to draw but also to enlarge the child's spirit through an appreciation of beauty. Seegmiller's own prints are an amalgam of Eastern influences, decorative understatement, and delicate beauty, and show a marked adherence to Dow's principles of design.

Bror Nordfeldt studied color woodcut with Frank Morley Fletcher at the Oxford Extension College in Reading in 1900. His earliest woodcuts exemplify Fletcher's teaching with their delicate handling of complex color schemes and a close adherence to Japanese *ukiyo-e* technique, including the use of the overlaying key block. He rightly took credit for helping to introduce this type of printmaking to America, writing, "I . . . was one of the first men in America to make prints by that method. . . . Indeed, the only person that was then using that method in this country was Arthur Dow."[31] Like Dow, Nordfeldt was interested in exploiting the creative potential of the woodblock print, going far beyond its reproductive uses.

In 1904, a year after Dow's departure, Jane Berry Judson arrived at Pratt from the small upstate New York town of Castile. Dow's principles were still being taught at Pratt, and it is easy to see from Judson's prints that she absorbed and practiced his lessons in composition and design. Like Nordfeldt, she later went to England where she studied color printmaking with Fletcher's friend and colleague Allen W. Seaby (the author of *Colour Printing with Linoleum and Wood Blocks,* 1925, an artist's how-to book that, like Dow's in the United States, attracted a wide audience in Britain). Upon her return to the States she went back to Castile, exhibiting regularly and holding memberships in the Rochester Art Club, the Buffalo Society of Artists, and the Print Club of Philadelphia. Her prints, inspired by Japanese woodcuts, are, like Dow's, intimate portraits of the rural area around her hometown.

Through Dow's teaching, many of his ideas traveled afar. In California, where many of his colleagues and students went to teach, his ideas were widely known and practiced. Of the three Gearhart sisters, Edna and May had studied with Dow in New York, while Frances had spent five summers studying printmaking with Charles Woodbury and Henry R. Poore (though she probably learned to make color woodcuts from May).[32] May also studied at the Art Institute of Chicago and with Hans Hofmann and Rudolph Schaeffer. All three sisters taught in the Los Angeles public school system, and May was ultimately named supervisor of art, a position she held from 1903 to 1939. Of the three, only Frances specialized in woodcut, though she often worked and exhibited with May. Edna is best represented by her drawings, and May by her color etchings.

In early 1904 Dow was hired to head the Art Department at Teachers College Columbia University. For the school year 1914–15, he enlisted

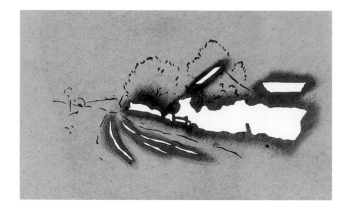

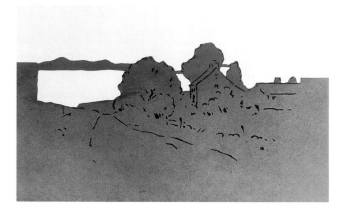

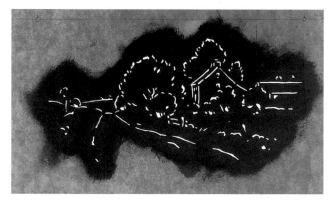

Stencil designs cut by Dow from shellacked mulberry paper. Dow frequently made stencils such as these to create simple prints. Collection George and Barbara Wright

the Czechoslovakian artist Vojtěch Pressig, whose specialty was linocut, to teach printing and book arts. (In December 1914 the Montclair Art Museum mounted an exhibition of Dow's woodcuts and Pressig's linocuts.) And, more famously, in 1907 he hired the novice instructor Clarence H. White to teach photography. Among Dow's students at Teachers College were Pedro de Lemos, who eventually had an ambitious career as art teacher in Berkeley and head of Stanford University's art museum; Margaret and Mary Frances Overbeck, two of the four sisters who later founded Overbeck Pottery; and the young avant-garde painter Georgia O'Keeffe. Although William S. Rice did not study with Dow, he was profoundly influenced by Dow's work at this time, as he frequently acknowledged. Rice's first encounter with Japanese color woodcuts came at the 1915 Pan Pacific Exposition in San Francisco; he later wrote a manual for use in art schools that incorporated many of the principles in Dow's *Composition.* As a skilled printmaker, Rice understood the demands of the medium well when he wrote, "To be a successful wood engraver one must have soul, imagination, deftness, ideas and knowledge; also unlimited patience."[33]

In Chicago, Mary Scovel, a Pratt graduate, established a curriculum based on Dow's theories at the Art Institute around 1900. Bertha Lum, a Californian who spent much of her time living abroad—first in Japan, then in China—and who made prints with great skill and intelligence, probably first encountered Dow's ideas while a student at the Art Institute of Chicago. Lum taught herself to make woodcut prints in 1903, using Dow's textbook and articles available in craftsman's magazines of the time. When she returned to Japan in 1907, she took professional printmaking lessons. The Boston tonalist painter Herman Dudley Murphy, a friend of both Denman Ross and Dow, also arrived in Chicago around the same time, accompanied by Albert Herter, and began to give private lessons in the synthetic method. Finally, Charles R. Ashbee, then the leading proponent of the British arts and crafts movement, was in residence at Jane Addams's Hull House in Chicago, where Dow himself gave a talk on March 21, 1900, as part of an extensive lecture tour of the Midwest.

Even in the South, where there were fewer art schools, Dow's teachings were popular. South Carolina artist Alice Ravenel Huger Smith was largely self-taught, though she attended drawing and painting classes at the Carolina Art Association and corresponded with printmakers Helen Hyde and Bertha Jaques. In 1910 she met the landscape artist Birge Harrison, the only artist she claims influenced her work. Smith fell in love with the Japanese prints that she found in a museum in her hometown of Charleston, and it was those prints—and possibly a knowledge of Dow's *Composition*—that shaped her softly poetic images of the South. Composed in the manner of a Dow exercise, her prints fill their confines and are eloquent despite their small size. And like Dow, Smith chose her subjects from her immediate surroundings, in her case, marshes, rice fields, and beaches in changing light and weather.

Among the printmakers influenced by Dow,

certain motifs emerge again and again. Often, they are motifs that were also dear to the *ukiyo-e* designers, particularly landscapes that are based not on a realistic depiction of nature but on the artist's interpretation of nature. Indigenous flora and fauna, in any size or shape, were also popular and could be rendered compositionally interesting within the prescribed format. Day lilies, water lilies, irises, and trees, particularly the graceful weeping willow, were some of the favorite subjects. Figurative work, though less often attempted, was also stylized and abstracted, with little relation to realism. The fact that these same forms recur in a variety of arts and crafts products—from ceramics to textiles to prints and photographs—enabled collectors to establish fully integrated arts and crafts environments.

THE BYRDCLIFFE CONNECTION

The dream of the total arts and crafts environment pervaded Byrdcliffe, a utopian community in Woodstock, New York, founded in 1903 by Ralph Whitehead, a wealthy follower of the ideas of William Morris and John Ruskin. Dow sent many of his best students to Byrdcliffe, and he supported Whitehead's plan to establish an artists' colony dedicated to a socialist ideal of shared community service. Like Dow, Whitehead firmly believed in beauty and pleasure in pure craftsmanship, in the creation of something utilitarian yet decorative, and the marriage of the everyday with the sublime.[34] In his "A Plea for Manual Labor," Whitehead stressed that "the pleasure of doing good work under healthy conditions, be it with a spade or with a sculptor's chisel,—the joy of a man in the work of his hands,—is not a mere passing satisfaction, but is an element in all sane life."[35]

Whitehead developed the plan for his artists' cooperative in conjunction with artist Bolton Brown, then teaching at Stanford University, and writer Hervey White, at that time associated with Hull House. Originally Santa Barbara was to be the site of this new venture, but after Whitehead had an affair that caused a minor scandal in the community, the three decided to look further afield for their ideal site. They sought a rural setting with easy access to a metropolitan area to provide the artists with a ready market for their products. After exploring several possible locations, Brown found the town of Woodstock and convinced the others of its appropriateness. Though near New York City, it retained a bucolic atmosphere; it was isolated enough to compel the colony to be somewhat self-sufficient yet close enough to the city to offer contacts with other artists, collectors, and galleries.

Once established, Byrdcliffe was fully equipped with a metal-working shop, a pottery, a woodworking shop, painting studio, dairy, library, guest house, artists' studios, and the main house, Whitehead's home, called White Pines. Among the master craftsmen hired to teach at Byrdcliffe were Herman Dudley Murphy, a painter of luminist Whistlerian landscapes and a framemaker, who headed the painting department[36]; Giovanni Battista Troccoli, an instructor in furniture making; and Edith Penman and Elizabeth Hardenburgh, who signed on to teach ceramics.

All were members of the Society of Arts and Crafts in Boston. With Dow's *Ipswich Prints* in mind, Whitehead also established a printing press at Byrdcliffe, and hired John Duncan, a Chicago artist who had set up a press at Jane Addams's Hull House, to teach printmaking.

During the early years of Byrdcliffe, Dow advised on the curriculum. But the first few seasons were rough. Murphy resigned at the end of the first year, and Birge Harrison, the noted tonalist landscape painter, was hired to replace him; he was joined by painters John Enneking and Paul Connoyer.[37] Then, after only two seasons at Byrdcliffe, Hervey White also left the community, fed up with Whitehead's autocratic management. White later established his own arts community nearby, called Maverick, based more on the principles of Walt Whitman than those of John Ruskin.

Yet, Byrdcliffe attracted many other artists and writers. Laurin Martin and Bertha Thompson, both members of the Society of Arts and Crafts in Boston, taught at the school. Martin specialized in light metalwork, while metalsmith Edward Thatcher continued to produce heavier hardware. Thompson taught jewelry making, and Marie Little, an artist from Virginia, made weavings that inspired Whitehead and his wife to take up the craft themselves. The illustrators Joseph and Frank Leyendecker came to Byrdcliffe with their sister, Augusta, who was studying sculpture. Artist and illustrator Edward Penfield, an old friend of the Whiteheads, also visited, as did the feminist reformers Charlotte Perkins Gilman and Jane Addams, friends of White's from Hull House.

Even C. R. Ashbee himself visited in 1915, but apparently he went away unimpressed.

Some of these participants had peripheral relationships with Dow while others knew him quite well. Before her marriage, Jane Whitehead had attended classes at the Académie Julian at the time Dow was there (though it is not known whether they met; classes were strictly segregated). Dow and Birge Harrison actually studied under the same instructors at the Académie Julian in the 1880s. And Dow also knew Murphy through various associations in the Boston art scene. Byrdcliffe artisans Edward Thatcher, George Eggers, Harry Stuart Michie, Edna Walker, and Zulma Steele had all studied under Dow at Pratt Institute, and Thatcher and Michie also worked with him when they were both on the faculty of Teachers College. Dow understood and appreciated what Whitehead was attempting with his Woodstock experiment, and the students he sent there thrived, applying the skills and design sense he had taught them in new ways.[38]

While not an advocate of the Ruskinian teachings at Byrdcliffe, Dow always felt that his students could benefit from time spent at Whitehead's colony. Thatcher, a 1902 design graduate from Pratt Institute, went to Byrdcliffe to work in the forge.[39] Between 1903 and 1905, he designed drawer pulls and other hardware for furniture produced at Byrdcliffe. After the furniture shop closed, he continued to spend summers at Byrdcliffe, teaching metalcraft, making jewelry, and publishing books on toys and ship models.

Another graduate from Pratt Institute was painter and printmaker George Eggers, who went

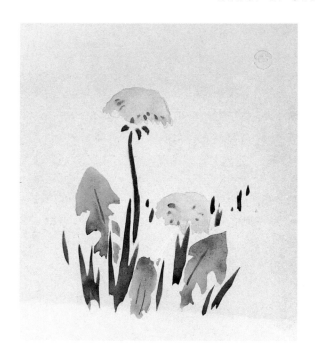

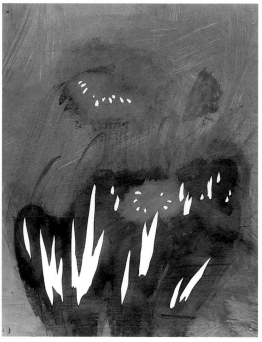

Floral stencil designs made by Dow. Collection George and Barbara Wright

to Byrdcliffe the first season, and later became a prominent museum director at the Art Institute of Chicago and the Denver Art Museum. Canadian artist Harry Stuart Michie had studied with Dow at Pratt, the Ipswich Summer School of Art, and Columbia. Like Dow, Michie collected Japanese art and textiles from many different cultures, which he later used in his own teaching. He was proficient in lettering, printing, woodworking, metalworking, and textiles, and his work reflected a strong Japanese aesthetic, inherited from his training with Dow.[40]

Two 1903 Pratt graduates, Edna Walker and Zulma Steele, came to Byrdcliffe the first year to make drawings for furniture.[41] Under Whitehead's supervision, and true to the teachings of Ruskin, they made careful watercolor studies of local flora and fauna: mountain laurel, pink azalea, dogwood, chestnut and apple blossoms, tiger lilies, iris, and leaf and berry designs. These stylized studies of natural elements were then incorporated into their furniture designs. After Whitehead's approval, the designs were handed over to the furniture shop foreman, Fordyce Herrick. Most of the furniture was created from indigenous woods such as poplar or quartered oak, and, for the first two summers at least, most of the carving was done by the head cabinetmaker, Riulf Erlandson, a Norwegian artist. When the furniture was complete, Steele and Walker stained or applied a finish to the pieces and sometimes painted the uncarved panels. All extant furniture from Byrdcliffe is dated 1904, with a carved lily insignia (Whitehead's trademark), but pieces were made throughout the three-year tenure of the woodworking shop, from 1903 to 1905. With his

ambitious plans to make Byrdcliffe self-sufficient through its furniture manufacture, Whitehead had not counted on the expense of the enterprise, which made the cost of purchasing a Byrdcliffe cabinet prohibitive to all but the wealthy. And unfortunately for sales, the beautifully designed and crafted furniture harked back to the chunky medieval designs of William Morris at a time when the market preferred the lighter, more sensuous art nouveau style.[42]

THE DECORATIVE AND THE UTILITARIAN

Dow's influence on the decorative arts continued to blossom in the first decade of the twentieth century. His classes at Ipswich and Pratt Institute offered students practical training in design and composition. At Columbia he steadily increased the number of decorative arts courses, and in 1912 the School of Practical Arts was established there, with courses in decorative arts, applied arts, and domestic science. Batik, tie and dye, stenciling, and block printing for textiles were the key components of class work. The fact that many of Dow's decorative arts students used his principles to teach these crafts throughout the country vastly extended his growing authority.

One of Dow's supporters was the powerful editor and publisher Joseph M. Bowles, who, in 1895, had used one of Dow's images of Ipswich as the cover of his magazine *Modern Art* (p. 14). In 1899 he also published the first edition of Dow's *Composition*. When Bowles and his wife, metalworker Janet Payne Bowles, settled in New York in 1907, their presence stimulated the already lively decorative arts community. Both were actively involved in the National Society of Craftsmen (established in 1906) and the National League of Handicraft Societies (founded in 1907), groups for which Dow served as vice-president. At the National League, Dow shared the position with Madeline Yale Wynne, a Chicago-based metalcrafter.[43] Although Janet Payne Bowles's own artwork bears little resemblance to Dow's, she followed many of his principles, stressing balance, rhythm, and function in both her work and her teaching. Like Dow, she rejected symmetry and machine fabrication. As a result, her metalwork has a naturalistic, handcrafted look, with nods to both the Celtic Revival and cubism.

Bowles's prominence as a metalsmith reflected the dramatic infusion of women into the decorative arts at the turn of the century. Women flocked to programs like Dow's that provided practical training in ceramics, china painting, textile design, wallpaper design, book binding, illustration, and rug design. In 1899 Katherine L. Smith had noted, "There is perhaps no truer form of art than the work that awaits women in this field where the artistic becomes the practical and everyday life is gladdened by some manifestations of the art crafts."[44]

An important example of this movement was Newcomb Pottery, established at H. Sophie Newcomb College in New Orleans in 1895. As part of a women's college, Newcomb Pottery was created to provide training and gainful employment for its graduates. Besides ceramics, the female artisans worked in linens, bookbinding, and metalwork. Almost all of their designs were based on the flora and fauna of the bayou region—

rice, cotton, magnolias, horsetail weeds, and wild geese. Each design was unique, and was supervised by Mary Given Sheerer, codirector of the program, who came from Cincinnati and was familiar with many of the Rookwood potters. For several decades, Sheerer, along with Joseph Meyer, the clay shop technician, oversaw the entire output of the Newcomb Pottery.[45] But many of the design concepts were directly attributable to Dow. At the turn of the century, an anonymous donor had given scholarships to Newcomb students to study at Dow's Ipswich Summer School of Art. Between 1900 and 1906 several students, as well as Sheerer, traveled north to study design and composition with Dow, whose ideas they incorporated into their work. In addition, a copy of Dow's *Composition* was available in the Newcomb library and served as a kind of bible to the design students.[46]

One of the leading women in the field of arts and crafts ceramics at the time was Adelaide Alsop Robineau, who had taught herself china painting because it was considered a genteel occupation for a working woman. She later studied painting with William Merritt Chase at his Shinnecock School on Long Island, and, in 1899, with support from her husband, she began publication of the magazine *Keramic Studio*, which influenced a generation of pottery designers with its clear illustrations and how-to instructions. In 1901 Robineau, Marshal Fry, and others took lessons with Dow. This may have been arranged through Fry who was a colleague of Dow's at Pratt.

Just down the road from Dow's summer school in Ipswich was the Marblehead Pottery, which was inspired by Dow's mandate and was under the

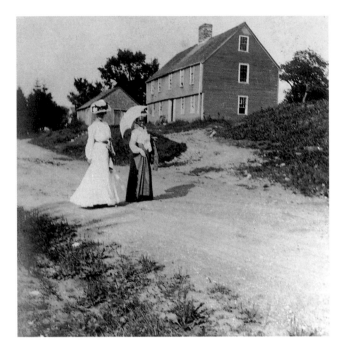

Emerson House, Ipswich. Dow used this building for his summer classes.
Collection George and Barbara Wright

Also near Dow's school was the Dedham Pottery, where Hugh Robertson directed the making of mostly blue-and-white wares. Denman Ross is credited with creating several of these designs, but in a Dedham pamphlet from around 1898 there is also a listing for a "Poppy. Dow' 2 Ways."[47] And there is little doubt that the Grueby Pottery in Boston was also influenced by Dow. William Henry Grueby and his business manager, William Hagerman Graves, were both members of the Saint Botolph's Club in Boston and may have been aware of Dow as early as 1890, when he exhibited his painting *Dewey Morning* there. Dow exhibited extensively in Boston in the early 1890s, showing works at Chase Galleries, the Paint and Clay Club, the Society of American Artists, and the Boston Art Club. It is probable that he came into contact with many of the leading Boston artists in this way.

Margaret and Mary Frances Overbeck, who later formed Overbeck Pottery with two of their sisters, studied with Dow at Columbia. It was Margaret's idea to establish a pottery in their home in Cambridge City, Indiana, though she died before the plan came to fruition. In 1911 Elizabeth, Hannah, and Mary Frances founded the Overbeck Pottery, which remained in existence until Mary Frances's death in 1955. All four sisters were active contributors to Robineau's *Keramic Studio*. From the beginning, Margaret, Hannah, and Mary Frances provided the majority of the designs for the pottery, while Elizabeth managed the more technical aspects, including the developing of glazes and clay mixtures. Throughout the forty-four years of the pottery's

direction of Arthur E. Baggs. Baggs was a graduate of the New York State School of Clayworking and Ceramics at Alfred University, which had been established in 1900 by Charles Fergus Binns, formerly of the Worcester Royal Porcelain Company, as the first college level ceramics program in the country. Many important ceramists studied at Alfred, including Paul Cox, who later became a technician at Newcomb Pottery; Elizabeth Overbeck, who later formed Overbeck Pottery with three of her sisters; and Frederick E. Walrath. Lillie Tourtellotte, a 1900 Pratt graduate, and Marshal Fry taught design at Alfred, and passed along Dow's views on the elements of composition to interested ceramics students.

existence, the sisters managed to keep their designs current, ranging from stylized naturalistic forms in the early years to art deco abstractions in the 1930s, and all were unique.

The New York Society of Keramic Arts included many of Dow's followers. Among them were Fry, Robineau, and Maud Mason, all of whom had studied with Dow in 1901. Edith Penman and Elizabeth Hardenburgh, who taught ceramics at Byrdcliffe, were also members, as was Charles Volkmar, who was actively involved with the National Society of Craftsmen, where Dow was vice president. Volkmar's son, Leon, taught at Pratt Institute with Dow until 1903, the year Dow left to begin his trip around the world.

Many of Dow's students and colleagues moved West, carrying his ideas to a receptive audience in the California arts and crafts movement. Isabelle Percy West, who had studied with Dow at Teachers College, used his design principles at the California School of Arts and Crafts, which she helped found in 1907. Anna Hills, a noted landscape painter who studied privately with Dow in New York, was the founder of the Laguna Beach Art Association and president of the California Art Club. Ralph Johonnot, a colleague of Dow's at Pratt, settled in Pacific Grove and taught painting and composition privately while maintaining an artists' supply shop in Carmel throughout the 1930s. And Ernest Batchelder, a New Englander best remembered for his ceramic tiles, opened the School of Design and Handicraft in Pasadena in 1909. A student at the Massachusetts Normal Art School, the Birmingham School of Arts and Crafts in England, and of Denman Ross at the

Harvard Summer School of Design, Batchelder incorporated Dow's design principles into his own work in ceramic tiles, enameling, and metalwork.

Another California metalworker and teacher indebted to Dow was Rudolf Schaeffer. He learned of Dow's principles through his teachers at the Thomas Normal Training School in Detroit, and later through Johonnot, who gave Schaeffer his first copy of *Composition*. Schaeffer taught at the California School of Arts and Crafts briefly before opening his own school in San Francisco, which ran from 1926 to 1984, when the artist was nearly a hundred years old. Schaeffer's work is simple in design, emphasizing the inherent beauty of the metal. The little ornamentation he allows is, not surprisingly, a subtle stylization of natural elements. Of Dow's influence, Schaeffer wrote: "In my teaching and critiques I emphasized the creative reasoning principles as set forth in Dow's 'Composition.' I found the succinct terms: subordination, repetition, transition, etc. universal in their application and if followed led the aesthetic expresion [*sic*] of one's intuition always into a unified whole. . . . The Dow principles are the backbone of the design and color teaching of the Rudolph Schaeffer School. . . . Styles and trends and materials and objectives change but the principles because of their universality never change."[48]

Finally, though their work is quite different, there are many similarities between Dow's background and that of Arthur Mathews, the leader of the California arts and crafts movement. Like Dow, Mathews studied at the Académie Julian in

Paris under Boulanger and Lefèbre from 1885 to 1889. During their time in Paris, both artists developed strong affinities with the works of Puvis de Chavannes and James McNeill Whistler. Like Dow, Mathews rejected his academic training. He became a noted art teacher, working at the Mark Hopkins Institute (which later became the California School of Fine Arts) in San Francisco from 1890 to 1906. After the 1906 earthquake destroyed much of the city, Mathews and his wife, Lucia, went into partnership with John Ziele, designing and manufacturing furniture at the Furniture Shop. Their style, known as the California Decorative Style, was related more to art nouveau and the Pre-Raphaelites than to the Eastern influences that pervade Dow's work.[49]

By 1911 Dow students filled many of the positions at the Los Angeles Normal School and in the Detroit school system, where Freer, Dow's influential friend, had turned the city into a Dow camp by the early 1900s. Freer wrote in support of a Dow student's application, "Professor Dow is unquestionably the foremost American in art education and his graduates now working in public and private schools are accomplishing great good."[50] In 1922, a group of former Dow students formed the Dow Association in Los Angeles, which by 1926 was a national organization with its own publication and series of exhibitions.

Besides his heavy teaching load at Columbia, Dow lectured extensively throughout the country. In 1909 he gave a lecture series at John Hopkins University and taught a lecture course for the National Society of Craftsmen in New York. In 1917 he spoke on Japanese art for the Trowbridge

Lecture series at Yale, illustrating his talk with fine examples from Charles Freer's collection. That same year he presented a popular summer seminar in Portland, Oregon. Whenever he traveled he met with former students who were teaching throughout the country and often gave lectures to their students. He was also instrumental in establishing the College Art Association and served as its director in 1912 and 1913. In 1918 a former pupil, Miss Margaret L. Baugh, of West Chester, Pennsylvania, left fifty thousand dollars in her will to promote Dow's educational system. This money was to be used specifically for non-academic teaching.

PHOTOGRAPHY AS A FINE ART

In the first decade of the century, photography had much in common with the arts and crafts aesthetic, encouraging both a return to nature and an emphasis on handcrafting by the artist. Artists like Dow accepted photography as a legitimate artistic form and were not put off by its mechanical aspect. An amateur photographer and an active member of the Boston Camera Club, Dow used his photographs as studies for paintings and as independent images. His photographs were often made as exercises in light and dark tonalities, experiments in his study of *notan*. In this regard, photography was especially useful, since the negative could, like a woodblock, be manipulated and printed in many variations.

Dow's interest in Japanese prints and his theories of patterning design and composition found great favor with pictorialist photographers. In their moody photographs, the pictorialists emulated painters such as Whistler, the Pre-Raphaelites, and the members of the Munich Secession, artists associated with a Japanese aesthetic and the arts and crafts movement. In composing his great photograph *Flat-Iron* (1902–03), for example, pictorialist Alfred Stieglitz "worked with blocks of tone in relation to each other, in the Whistlerian manner, thinking in terms of the total design rather than individual objects against a neutral background."[51] The result is a carefully balanced composition in which muted tones of black and white create an air of mystery. As the influential critic Charles Caffin argued, it was imperative for the pictorialist photographer to understand "the laws of composition, those also affect the distribution of light and shade; his eye must be trained to distinguish 'values,' that is to say, the varying effect of light upon objects of different material and the gradual changes in the color of an object according as it is nearer to or farther from the eye . . . in addition there must be the instinctive sense of what is beautiful in line and form and color, which may be developed by study, and, lastly, the natural gift of imagination which conceives a beautiful subject and uses technique and instinct to express it."[52] These aesthetic criteria clearly echo the main lines of Dow's *Composition*.

Among the many pictorialists influenced by Dow's theories was Gertrude Käsebier, who studied with Dow at Pratt for a year after her graduation in 1895. At the end of that year she had her first exhibition, at the Boston Camera

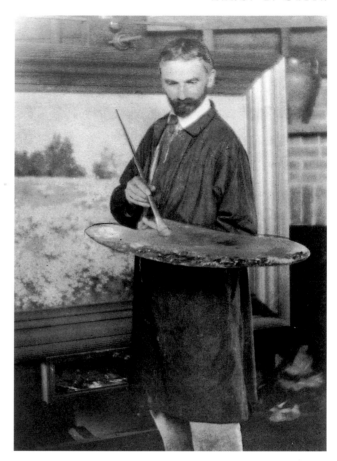

Dow painting in his studio, ca. 1905. Collection George and Barbara Wright

Club, probably through Dow's influence. In 1899 Dow and Joseph T. Keiley wrote favorable reviews of Käsebier's work for *Camera Notes,* and in the first issue of Stieglitz's *Camera Work* in 1903 her dreamlike photographs were prominently featured. In discussing Käsebier's work, Dow wrote, "A picture is indeed a representation of something, but when produced by a real artist it has more than representation. Its tones, colors, shapes, its composition and style, the power and grace of its execution, all combine to make it a work of beauty, a work of fine art."[53]

Käsebier also encouraged her young studio assistant, Alvin Langdon Coburn, to study with Dow. Coburn, a distant cousin of F. Holland Day, had probably already heard of the Pratt instructor. He studied first with Day, in 1900, and the following year with Robert Demachy and Edward Steichen in Paris. In 1902 and 1903, the same years he worked in Käsebier's New York studio, Coburn enrolled in Dow's summer courses at Ipswich. There he learned about abstract relations between spaces, the setting of one tone against another, and the careful arrangement of shapes. As he later wrote, "At the Summer School we were taught painting, pottery, and wood-block prints, and I also used my camera, for Dow had the vision, even at that time, to recognize the possibilities of photography as a medium of personal artistic expression. I learned many things at this school, not least an appreciation of what the Orient has to offer us in terms of simplicity and directness."[54] A photographic prodigy, Coburn was elected to the Brotherhood of the Linked Ring and the Photo-Secession in 1903, when he was only twenty-one. Eventually he set up his own photographic studio in London and became known not only for his lush gum platinum prints but for his staunch advocacy of photography as an art. Printing his negatives on platinum paper, then coating the prints with layers of pigmented gum like a painting, Coburn achieved a visually rich texture that became his signature.

Edward Steichen, though neither a student nor a colleague of Dow's, followed many of the precepts of Dow's ideas on composition. Strongly influenced by the work of Whistler, Steichen was an enthusiastic and talented painter, printmaker, and photographer. In 1899, at the age of twenty, he submitted three photographs to the second Philadelphia Salon. Clarence H. White, who was one of the jurors, was so impressed with Steichen's work that he wrote to him personally, and gave him a letter of introduction to Stieglitz, who was equally enthralled. The following year Steichen set off for Paris, where, like Dow, he enrolled at the Académie Julian. But, disgusted with the academic system, Steichen stayed only a few weeks, though he remained in France for two more years and became active in avant-garde circles. His photographs from this time were often purposely shot out of focus and printed with a gum process that produced a grainy, homemade quality. Like Coburn, Steichen often brushed the gum directly onto the surface of the print, controlling the development of the image manually as well as chemically. In this way, he was able to carefully synthesize form, space, and tone to create the sort of moody landscapes that Dow advocated in *Composition*.

Joseph T. Keiley, who had trained as a lawyer, was an active member of the Photo-Secession and an articulate spokesman through his articles in *Camera Notes* and *Camera Work*. Though less adventurous than the other Photo-Secessionists in his own work, he was conscious of Dow's manual; he studied *Composition* with care, and his images attest to his successful experiments with the essentials of line, *notan*, and color.

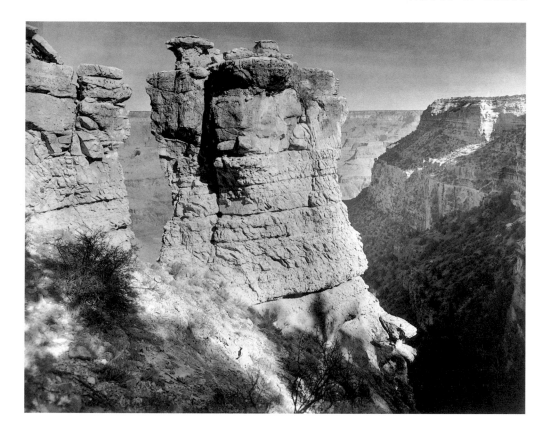

A Dow photograph of the Grand Canyon, probably from his 1911–12 trip with Alvin Langdon Coburn. Collection George and Barbara Wright

Though Dow had offered some photography instruction at Ipswich, he only incorporated it into his curriculum at Columbia in 1907, when he hired Clarence H. White to teach evening classes with fieldwork conducted on Saturdays.[55] White was considered by his colleagues to be a master photographer, but he had no prior teaching experience. Soon, however, he was highly sought after by students like Karl Struss, Amy Whittemore, and Francesca Bostwick. White also taught classes at the Brooklyn Institute of Arts and Sciences and at the Seguinland School of Photography in Maine before founding the White School of Photography with artist Max Weber in

1914. Among his later students were Margaret Bourke-White, Laura Gilpin, Dorothea Lange, Paul Outerbridge Jr., Ralph Steiner, and Doris Ulmann, artists who had a major impact on the course of twentieth-century photography.

Although primarily a painter, Max Weber served as a key conduit between Dow, modernism, and the new status of photography. A student of Dow's at Pratt Institute, Weber began to excel during his second year, and, after graduation, he won a scholarship for an additional year of study with Dow.[56] Dow encouraged Weber to spend time studying in museums and to consider traveling abroad. In 1901 Weber took a teaching

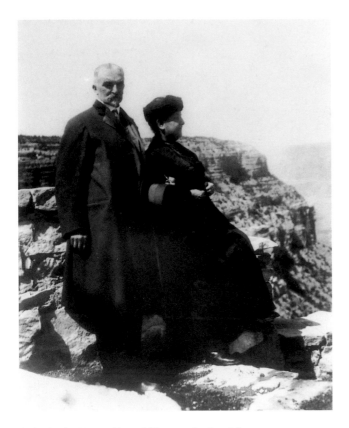

Arthur Wesley Dow and his wife Minnie at the Grand Canyon, 1919.
Collection George and Barbara Wright

ing modernists of the day—Pablo Picasso, Jean Metzinger, Maurice Denis, Albert Gleizes, and Sonia Delauney. He also formed a close friendship with the elderly "naive" painter Henri Rousseau. During the winter of 1907–08, he took private lessons with Matisse.

Upon his return to the United States in 1909, Weber became associated with Alfred Stieglitz, who gave him a show at 291 and published his art criticism in *Camera Work*. Weber, in turn, helped Stieglitz organize and hang the large and important exhibition of pictorialist photography shown at the Albright Art Gallery in Buffalo in 1910. Local photographers such as Wilbur Heber Porterfield and Augustus Thibaudeau were actively involved in the Buffalo component of this exhibition. While amateurs in one sense, they produced works of great beauty and harmony of tones. They were active in photographic circles and friends with the leading pictorialists, so it is not surprising that their work shows the same sensitivity to composition.

Stieglitz's autocratic selection of the Buffalo exhibition provoked a schism among the Photo-Secessionists, and Weber sided with White, Coburn, and Käsebier against Stieglitz. Later he taught art history and design composition at White's Seguinland School of Photography in Maine, and, after 1914, at the White School of Photography in Manhattan.

Writing of his admiration for Weber's work, Alvin Langdon Coburn later remarked, "Weber had a sense of design that never failed him, and what is equally important, a beauty of colour vision; therefore, however revolutionary his

position at the public high school in Lynchburg, Virginia, where he stayed two years, to save money for a trip to Europe. In 1903 he took a job as head of the Department of Art and Manual Training at the Minnesota State Normal School in Duluth, a position he held until 1905, when he finally had enough money together and he set sail for France. Like Dow, Weber enrolled at the Académie Julian in Paris, but it was the very unacademic work of Cézanne and Matisse that attracted him most forcefully. During his four years in Paris, Weber made friends with the lead-

ideas, he could not help producing pictures that have a lasting attraction."[57] Weber's pictures are, in a way, a sensitive amalgamation of all he had learned. They show that he learned to compose space, filling it in a thoughtful yet demanding way, and to look to the art of other cultures for inspiration. Weber remained loyal to Dow's theory of syntheticism, though he interpreted structure and space as a cubist and used the term "space filling" to teach the strictures of good composition. Weber was much more artistically innovative than Dow, but he never denigrated his first teacher. Indeed, he later wrote, "When I got to Paris in 1905 I was struck by the fact that Mr. Dow anticipated some of the aesthetic principles of art the Fauves had striven for only years later. Mr. Dow was one of the greatest art educators this country was blessed with."[58]

Karl Struss stands out as a key transitional figure to the next generation of photographers. Along with White, Käsebier, and Coburn, Struss was a founding member of the Pictorial Photographers of America in 1916, but even by then his work was changing radically. In 1919 Struss left New York for Hollywood, where he pursued a career in cinematography. Barbara Morgan, who had studied with Dow in New York and was a member of the Los Angeles Dow Association, went on to create memorable portrait studies of leading arts figures, most notably of Martha Graham. Another Californian, Imogen Cunningham, who was first inspired to pick up a camera after seeing the work of Gertrude Käsebier, became a founding member of the important photographic group f/64. For all of these artists,

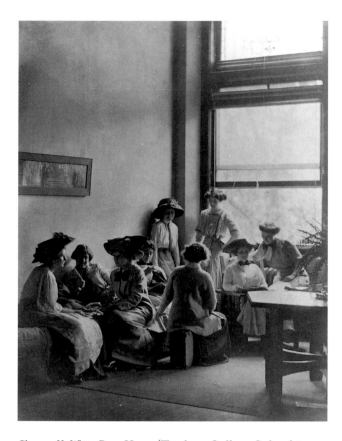

Clarence H. White, Rest Hour (Teachers College Columbia University), *1912. Possibly silver print, 9¾ × 7¾ inches. National Museum of American Art, Smithsonian Institution; museum purchase from the Charles Isaacs' Collection made possible in part by the Luisita L. and Franz H. Denghausen Endowment*

and many others as well, Dow's exhortation rings true: "The artist is able to bring to you an experience of beauty, because he is able to choose the best SPACING, the most harmonious RHYTHMS, the most mysterious TONE and COLOR." He continued, "The artist does not teach us to see facts: he teaches us to feel harmonies and to recognize supreme quality."[59]

Despite a fall from a horse in the Grand

Canyon in 1919, which weakened his constitution and made painting difficult, Dow remained indefatigable. He continued his always ambitious schedule of lecturing and teaching, until, on December 13, 1922, shortly after delivering a lecture, Dow suffered a heart attack and died.

CONCLUSION

Though Dow was instrumental in ushering modernism into the work of American artists, his own approach always remained conservative. His favorite European artists were Auguste Rodin, D'Espagnat, Paul Besnard, Charles Cazin, Puvis de Chavannes, Zuloaga, and, of course, the expatriate James McNeill Whistler. In his lectures on modernism, Dow only taught up to the work of Manet and Monet. Though he did not understand modernism in all its complications and rhetoric, he appreciated its rejection of academic teaching and its connections with music. Writing in the 1930s, Dow's friend and biographer Arthur Johnson noted that, "He knew both by instinct and by training that music was the purist of all the arts and was a sort of divine measuring stick to evaluate man's creative impulses."[60] In 1915, in an effort to stay abreast of the changing times, he added a course in modernist painting to the curriculum at Teachers College so that students could be informed about contemporary art.

In 1914 Dow's best-known student came to Teachers College to study with him. Though no longer at the forefront of art education, Dow still was able to inspire Georgia O'Keeffe with his concepts. She recognized and appreciated his passion: "This man had one dominating idea: to fill a space in a beautiful way—and that interested him. After all, everyone has to do just this—make choices—in his daily life, even when only buying a cup and saucer. By this time I had a technique for handling oil and watercolor easily; Dow gave me something to do with it."[61]

Dow's approach to art was universal; it could be translated by any artist into any form, based on a few simple principles. For him, composition was the key, the fundamental element of art making that was synonymous with individuality. Yet, he always maintained that composition was a learned skill, available to all:

> The study of composition means art education for the entire people, for every child can be taught to compose—that is, to know and feel beauty and to produce it in simple ways . . . In my experience, art instruction must begin by awakening the perceptions of beauty, by causing an exercise by choice and judgment, that reflects the personal thought or emotion of the student. The pupil makes several designs, chooses the best, compares them with similar things in the art world and is helped to perceive the style and distinction of really fine things. By continually exercising judgment and personal feelings, he gains creative ability. This simple beginning underlies painting, sculpture, architecture and decoration.[62]

Through his teaching, his writings, and the example of his own work, Dow made aesthetic appreciation and creativity an accessible option for everyone.

NOTES

1. Oscar Wilde, *The Selected Prose of Oscar Wilde* (London: Methuen & Co., Ltd., 1914); and as quoted in Thomas Verde, "Oscar Wilde in Bangor?" *Down East* 36, no. 3 (October 1989): 71.

2. Frank Lloyd Wright, "The Art and Craft of the Machine," *Brush and Pencil* (May 1901): 84.

3. Ibid., p. 77.

4. Arthur Warren Johnson, *Arthur Wesley Dow, Historian, Artist, Teacher* (Ipswich, Mass.: Ipswich Historical Society, 1934), p. 87.

5. Arthur Wesley Dow, *Composition: A Series of Exercises in Art Structure for the Use of Students and Teachers* (1899; repr. New York: Doubleday, Page and Co., Inc., 1913), p. 46.

6. Arthur Wesley Dow, "Talks on Appreciation of Art," *The Delineator* (January 1915): 15.

7. Advertising pamphlet for Dow's *Composition,* Dow Papers, Archives of American Art, Smithsonian Institution, Washington, D.C.

8. The *Ipswich Antiquarian Papers* was published over a period of five years, from 1879 to 1884, with many examples of Dow's illustrative work. These are mostly unembellished line images that have little to do with Dow's later printing successes.

9. Johnson, *Arthur Wesley Dow,* p. 34.

10. Arthur Wesley Dow, letter to Minnie Dow, February 26, 1890, quoted in ibid., p. 54.

11. Fenollosa's widow, Mary, described this friendship in her introduction to her husband's two volume *Epochs of Chinese and Japanese Art:* "While in the first enthusiastic stages of his work for a better system of art education in America, a new and very precious friendship was formed. This was with Mr. Arthur Wesley Dow, of Ipswich, Massachusetts, a young artist who had just returned from Paris. Literally the first moment in which he met Professor Fenollosa and was shown some of the great examples of Japanese Art, these two influences became clear factors in his life. On the other hand Professor Fenollosa found in this ardent and receptive young spirit the inspiration and encouragement for which he had been longing." (1913; repr. New York: Dover Publications 1963), p. xix.

12. Arthur Wesley Dow, "Notes for a lecture delivered before 1895 at a private Boston school," unpublished manuscript, Dow Papers, Archives of American Art, Smithsonian Institution, Washington, D.C.

13. Sylvester Koehler had been Louis Prang's technical manager for ten years before serving as curator at the U.S. National Museum (part of the Smithsonian). From 1887 until his death in 1900, he was curator of prints at the Museum of Fine Arts, Boston, and an invaluable resource for Dow in planning the technical aspects of his own work.

14. Johnson, *Arthur Wesley Dow,* p. 56.

15. Ralph Johonnot (1880–1940) taught at Pratt until 1909; he moved to Pacific Grove, California, in 1912, teaching art privately and maintaining an art supply store in Carmel during the 1930s. Grace Cornell was a Pratt graduate, class of 1899; she stayed on to teach there, and was later hired by Dow to teach at Teachers College Columbia University.

16. Circular for Ipswich Summer School of Art, Summer 1892. Dow Papers, Ipswich Historical Society.

17. In his 1903 analysis of the programs at the Ipswich Summer School of Art, author Sylvester Baxter argued for the advantage of the machine under certain conditions. Baxter imagined an "assembling of the workers in shops where ideal developments of motive-power, comfort, provisions for hygiene, hours of work, compensation, and beauty of surroundings, would obtain. By thus giving to the machine its due recognition, it is conceivable that the arts and crafts of Ipswich might become a powerful factor in the new industrial dispensation that must dawn for our world as our civilization seeks an equilibrium upon the new level established by the era of mechanical production and distribution." See Sylvester Baxter, "Handicraft, and Its Extension at Ipswich," *Handicraft* 1, no. 11 (February 1903): 268.

18. Quoted in Helmut Gernsheim and Alison Gernsheim, eds., *Alvin Langdon Coburn, Photographer: An Autobiography* (New York: Frederick A. Praeger, 1966), p. 22.

19. See Anna P. Brooks, "Arthur Wesley Dow: An Intimate Sketch," *Dark and Light,* no. 2 (March 1924): n.p.

20. Fletcher and Batten's first print was *Eve and the Serpent* (1896), cut from six blocks of cherry wood in an intricate design with an ambitious color scheme. In a letter to

The Studio (vol. 7, 1896), Batten described his process, which was slightly different from Dow's. Batten sized his Japanese paper with milk and ground his powdered pigments with a mixture of dextrine and glycerines. Fletcher went on to teach at University College, Reading, where he first introduced courses in color woodcut. In 1908 Fletcher moved to Edinburgh to take up the post of director of the newly founded Edinburgh College of Art; at his old friend Albert Herter's invitation, he left this position in 1923 to become director of the Santa Barbara School of the Arts. He later became an active member of the California Society of Printmakers (along with Frances Gearheart) and was named vice president in 1929.

21. Quoted in Mabel Key, "A New System of Art Education, Arranged and Directed by Arthur W. Dow" *Brush and Pencil* 4 (August 1899): 267.

22. Fenollosa went on to describe Dow's technique rather poetically: "Pigment washed upon the wood, and allowed to press the sheet with touch as delicate as a hand's caress, clings shyly only to the outer fibres, the hills of its new world, leaving the deep wells of light in the valleys, the whiteness of the paper's inner heart, to glow through it, and dilute its solid color with a medium of pure luminosity." Ernest Fenollosa, *Color Prints of Arthur Wesley Dow* (Boston: Alfred Mudge & Son, 1895), p. 5.

23. Dow, *Composition*, p. 38.

24. Arthur Wesley Dow, Japan diary, 1903, Dow Papers, Archives of American Art, Smithsonian Institution, Washington, D.C.

25. Peyton Boswell, "The New American School of Wood Block Printers in Color," *Art World* 9 (July 1918): 168.

26. Arthur Wesley Dow to Frederic Pratt, Sept. 12, 1895, Dow Papers, Archives of American Art, Smithsonian Institution, Washington, D.C.

27. Arthur Wesley Dow, "Some Results of a Synthetic Method of Art Instruction," *Pratt Institute Monthly* 6, no. 3 (December 1897): 71. Fenollosa never did take up his teaching post at Pratt; in 1895 he divorced his wife and married his assistant, which resulted in his return to Japan to live.

28. Edna Bel Boies scrapbook, November 1902–April 1903, p. 2, Edna Hopkins Papers, Archives of American Art,

Smithsonian Institution, Washington, D.C. In 1904, when Boies was visiting Japan on her honeymoon with husband James Hopkins, she studied some of the same masters as had Dow, possibly at his suggestion.

29. Margaret Jordan Patterson went to Pratt in 1895, probably at Dow's suggestion. She had known him in Boston where she most likely took private lessons with him, as well as with Charles Woodbury and Dow's friend Herman Dudley Murphy. After Pratt, she returned to Boston, though frequently traveling abroad, and became director of drawing for the Boston public schools.

30. Richard Whelan suggests that Georgia O'Keeffe may have been influenced by Smith's second show at 291 in early 1908. Both women relied on Dow's compositional principles and both shared "a preoccupation with trying to express in visual terms their reactions to music." Richard Whelan, *Alfred Stieglitz: A Biography* (New York: Da Capo Press, 1997), p. 373.

31. Nordfeldt, draft of letter, undated, Nordfeldt papers, Archives of American Art, Smithsonian Institution, Washington, D.C. In 1900 Nordfeldt had worked in Paris with Albert Herter, an old friend of Fletcher's who was creating murals for the Universal Exposition in Paris. It was probably at Herter's suggestion that Nordfeldt traveled to England to study printmaking with Fletcher. Like Dow, Fletcher taught color printmaking in the traditional manner to numerous students in the course of a long teaching career, first at Oxford Extension College in Reading, then at the Edinburgh Art School, and finally in Santa Barbara, California, where he moved in 1923. After completing his studies, Nordfeldt returned to his hometown of Chicago.

32. Ironically, Poore disparaged Dow's work as purely decorative, and published a refutation of Dow's ideas in his own treatise *Pictorial Composition* (1903). See Frederick C. Moffatt, *Arthur Wesley Dow, 1857–1922* (Washington, D.C.: Smithsonian Institution Press, 1977), p. 90.

33. William S. Rice, "Block-Printing a Revived Art," *Oakland Tribune,* October 21, 1917.

34. As Whitehead wrote, "It is too early yet to speak of our work at Byrdcliffe. When we have organized some small industries here; when we have proved that is possible to

combine with a simple country life many and varied forms of manual and intellectual activity; when we have made some furniture and woven some handmade textiles which can hold their own, the writer hopes to be permitted to give an account of our doings. . . . it is our intention to make furniture of a simple kind, which shall be good in proportion, and to which distinction may be given the application of color and of carving by artists' hands; that we intend to make a specialty of frames for pictures . . . that we hope to make a beginning of the truly democratic art of color-printing, by which work in colors of really artistic worth may be made accessible to those who cannot afford easel-pictures; and finally we will give a welcome to any true craftsmen who are in sympathy with our ideas and who will help us to realize them." See Whitehead, "A Plea for Manual Work," *Handicraft* 2, no. 3 (June 1903): 73.

35. Ibid., p. 72.

36. In an 1899 article, Dora Morrell described Murphy's teaching methods: "In principle and artistic intention Mr. Murphy is one of the active believers in a systematic progression in study which is as definitely scientific as a search for the beautiful can be, and to which Arthur W. Dow and Denman Ross have given their thought and study for many years." Dora Morrell, "Hermann Dudley Murphy," *Brush and Pencil* 5, no. 2 (November 1899): 57.

37. Birge Harrison studied with Boulanger and Lefèbre in Paris at the same time as Dow, so it is probable that they first met there. He was also the brother of Alexander Harrison, an artist who had greatly influenced Dow's early work in Pont Aven. In 1906 Birge Harrison left Byrdcliffe to become director of the Art Students League Summer School in Woodstock.

38. Alf Evers, *Woodstock: History of an American Town* (Woodstock, N.Y.: Overlook Press, 1987), pp. 427–28.

39. Alf Evers, *The Catskills: From Wilderness to Woodstock* (Garden City, N.Y.: Doubleday & Co., 1972), p. 624.

40. Marilee Boyd Meyer et al., *Inspiring Reform: Boston's Arts and Crafts Movement* (Wellesley, Mass.: Davis Museum and Cultural Center in association with Bulfinch Press/Little, Brown and Company, 1997), p. 224.

41. Evers, *The Catskills*, p. 624.

42. In upstate New York alone, three important furniture shops provided simple, well-made pieces at a reasonable price. Charles Rohlfs opened his Furniture Shop in Buffalo in 1898, designing beautifully crafted, one-off pieces, some with simple, Dow-like stylized designs. Gustav Stickley, whose name became synonymous with the clean, under-stated lines of oak mission furniture opened his shop, Gustav Stickley & Company, in Syracuse the same year. Harvey Ellis, who worked with Stickley for a period, moved on to Rochester where he shared studio space with former Dow student Louise Stowell. I am grateful to David Cather for bringing to my attention another connection between Stickley and Dow, the architect Lamont Warner, who had been a Dow student at Pratt Institute. In the early 1900s, after graduation, Warner worked as a designer for Stickley and then was hired by Dow to teach at Teachers College. Three years later, Elbert Hubbard's Roycroft Shop in East Aurora, New York, produced its first furniture for sale. The same year, 1902, Stickley began publication of *The Craftsman* to which many leading arts and crafts practitioners contributed.

43. Other important metalworkers were also associated with Dow. One of his Ipswich students, Antonio Cirino, co-authored *Jewelry Making and Design* (1917) with Augustus F. Rose of the Rhode Island School of Design. Rose himself was influenced by both Ross and Lauren Martin, who taught at Byrdcliffe and was an active member of the Society of Arts and Crafts, Boston. Josephine Hartwell Shaw (1865–1941) studied with Dow at Pratt and with Ross at the Harvard Summer School. And the jewelry maker Susan Leland Hill, who died in 1961, studied Dow's methods under Michie at Worcester and with Rose at the Rhode Island School of Design. See Meyer et al., *Inspiring Reform*.

44. Katherine Louise Smith, "Women in the Arts and Crafts," *Brush and Pencil* 5 (November 1899): 76.

45. Mary Given Sheerer, codirector of the program, came from the Cincinnati area and was familiar with many of the Rookwood potters. With great energy and discrimination, she made Newcomb her life's work.

46. Lotta Lee Troy, a bookbinder who studied with Dow at Columbia, joined the staff of Newcomb in 1909 as an instructor in bookbinding and design; when she retired

in 1940 she was professor of art and had served as director of the School of Art for nearly a decade. Also, in 1914, a small selection of Dow's paintings was mounted in the Newcomb College gallery, inspiring a new group of students, long after the Ipswich Summer School of Art had closed its doors.

47. This information was kindly provided to me by James Kaufman of the Dedham Historical Society. Kaufman also suggested that the design was probably not created by Dow himself but by Robertson, inspired by Dow. James Kaufman, letter to the author, March 28, 1998.

48. Rudolf Schaeffer to Frederick Moffatt, undated letter (ca. 1976), Oakland Museum Archives, Oakland, Calif.

49. On Mathews, see Harvey Jones, *Mathews: Masterpieces of the California Decorative Style* (Oakland, Calif.: Oakland Museum, 1985).

50. As quoted in Frederick Moffatt, "The Life and Times of Arthur Wesley Dow" (Ph.D. diss., University of Chicago, 1972), p. 235.

51. William Innes Homer, *Alfred Stieglitz and the American Avant-Garde* (Boston: New York Graphic Society, 1977), p. 22

52. Ibid., p. 10.

53. Arthur Wesley Dow, "Mrs. Gertrude Käsebier's Portrait Photographs from a Painter's Point of View," *Camera Notes* 3, no. 1 (July 1899): 22.

54. Quoted in Gernsheim and Gernsheim, eds., *Alvin Langdon Coburn,* p. 22. Dow and Coburn remained friends, corresponding on occasion. In the winter of 1911–12 they traveled together to photograph the natural splendors of the Grand Canyon, a trip that had a profound effect on both artists.

55. Dow first offered the position to Stieglitz, who suggested White for the position. It was another of Dow's students, Mary Ketcham, who, as director of the School of Visual and Performing Arts at Syracuse University in 1912, established the first college-level department of photography in the United States, under E. J. Wall, a member of the Royal Photographic Society of England.

56. Dow's initial reaction to Weber was that he was, at best, a lackluster student. But during his second year at Pratt Institute, Weber began to apply himself. He won a scholarship in 1899 that enabled him to stay on for an additional year after graduation to study with his mentor. Weber was trained as a master cabinetmaker at Pratt, so it is not surprising that in his later years he concentrated his printmaking efforts on woodcuts. See Ala Story, *Max Weber* (Santa Barbara: University of California at Santa Barbara, 1968).

57. Gernsheim and Gernsheim, eds., *Alvin Langdon Coburn,* p. 92.

58. Max Weber to Ethelwyn Putnam, October 30, 1958. Later, Weber reiterated, "As the years glide by, my affection and esteem augment. I never refrain from making it known that I consider him the greatest teacher I have had. He brought to our West the wisdom and aesthetic inspiration of the great Eternal East." Weber to Putnam, November 22, 1958, Dow Papers, Archives of American Art, Smithsonian Institution, Washington, D.C.

59. Dow, "Talks on the Appreciation of Art," p. 15.

60. Johnson, *Arthur Wesley Dow,* p. 83.

61. O'Keeffe, quoted in Katherine Kuh, ed., *The Artist's Voice* (New York: Harper and Row, 1962), p. 190.

62. Arthur Wesley Dow, quoted in Thomas Harrison Cumming, "Some Photographs by Alvin Langdon Coburn," *American Journal of Photography* 10, no. 3 (March 1903): 92.

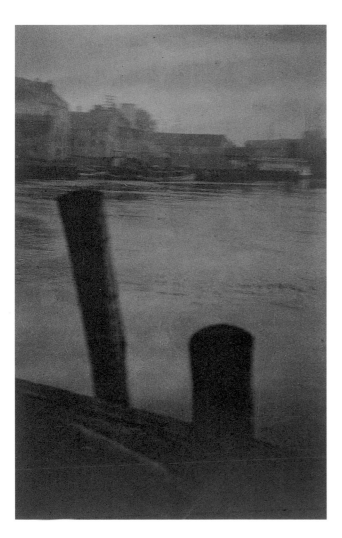

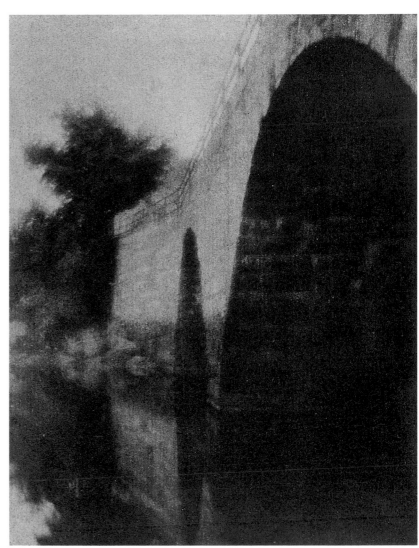

ALVIN LANGDON COBURN
The Pier, 1903

ALVIN LANGDON COBURN
The Bridge-Ipswich, 1904

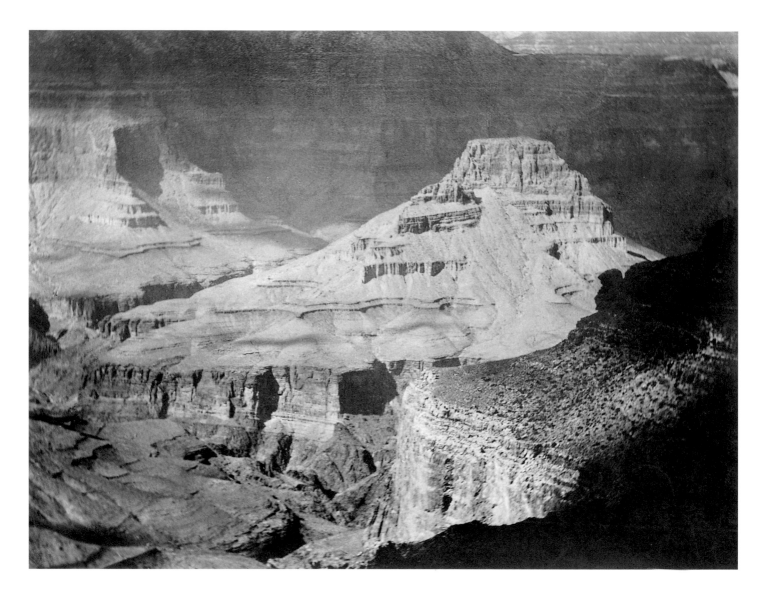

ALVIN LANGDON COBURN
Grand Canyon, 1912

ALVIN LANGDON COBURN ▶
Grand Canyon, 1912

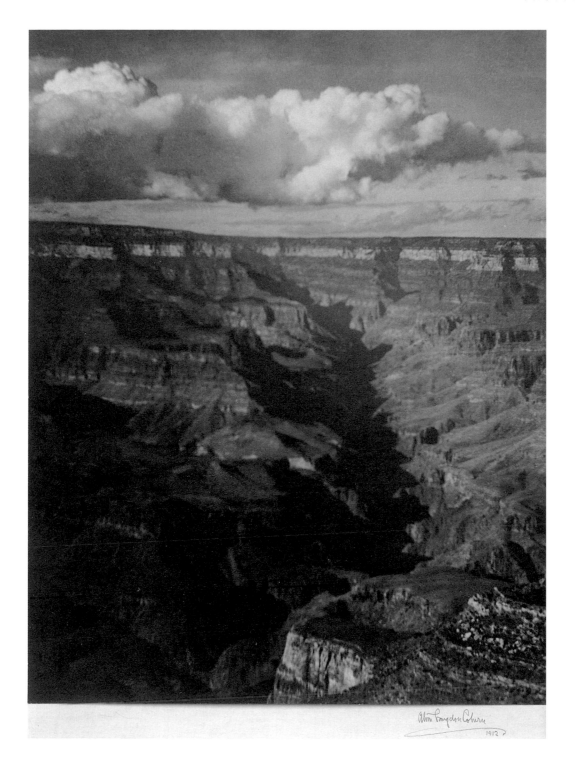

ARTHUR WESLEY DOW
Silhouetted Trees, ca. 1895–1910

ARTHUR WESLEY DOW ▶
On Yavapai Trail, 1911

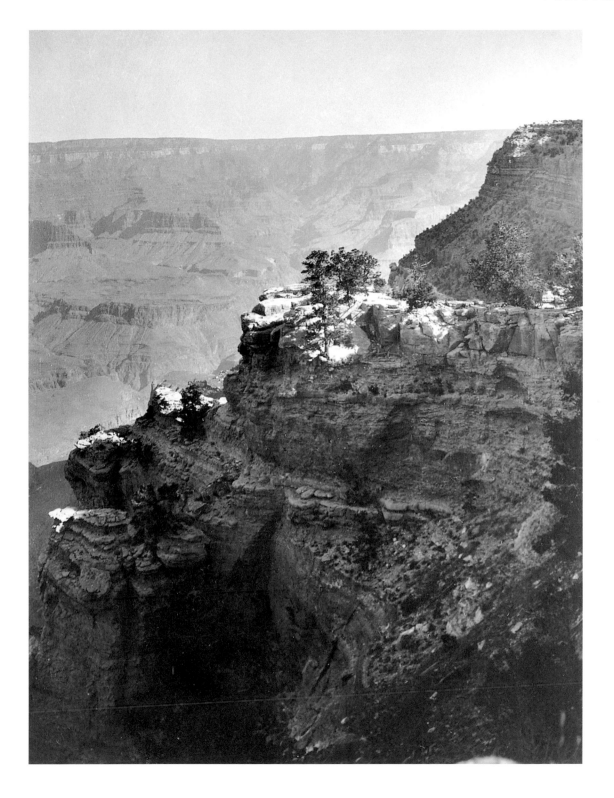

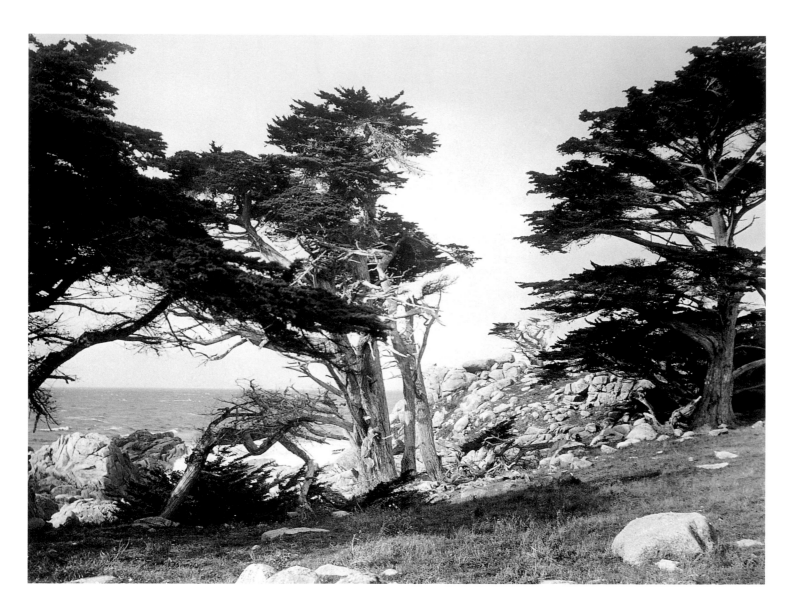

ARTHUR WESLEY DOW
Pacific Grove, 1912

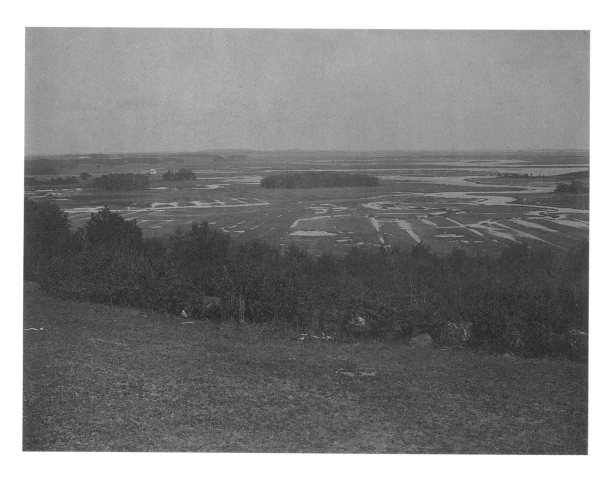

ARTHUR WESLEY DOW
The Dragon, n.d.

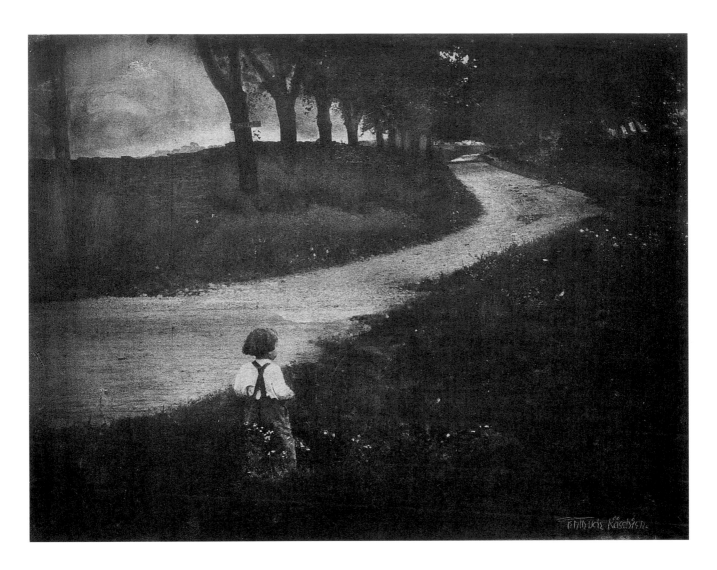

GERTRUDE KÄSEBIER
The Road to Rome, 1903

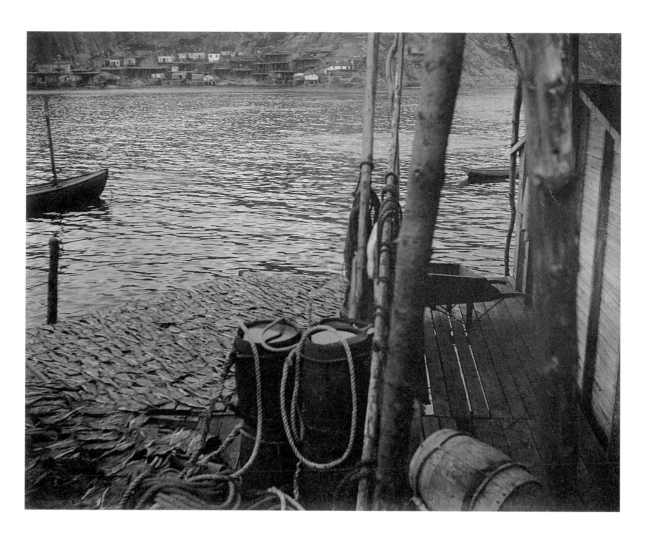

GERTRUDE KÄSEBIER
Fishing Banks: Newfoundland, 1912

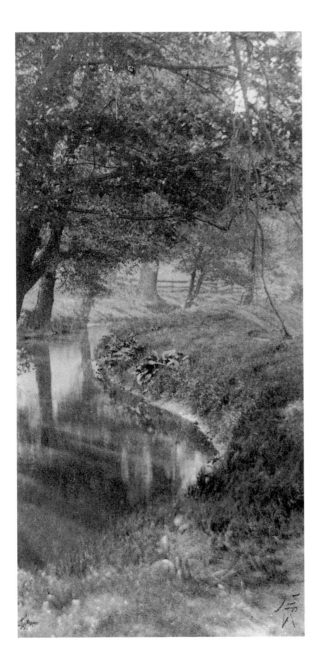

JOSEPH T. KEILEY
Landscape, ca. 1900

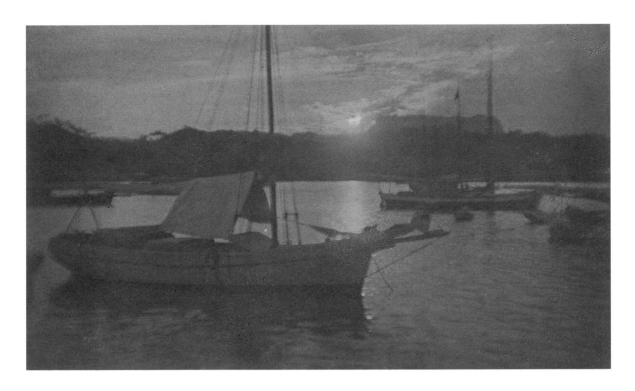

JOSEPH T. KEILEY
Reverie: The Last Hour, 1901

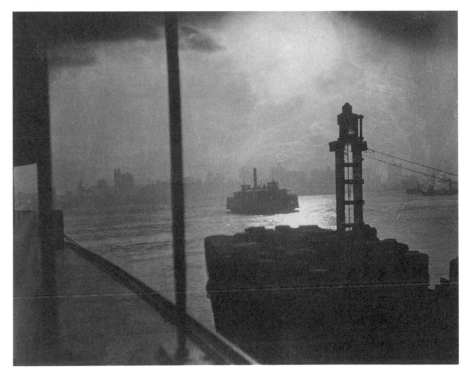

JOSEPH T. KEILEY
From a New York Ferryboat, 1904

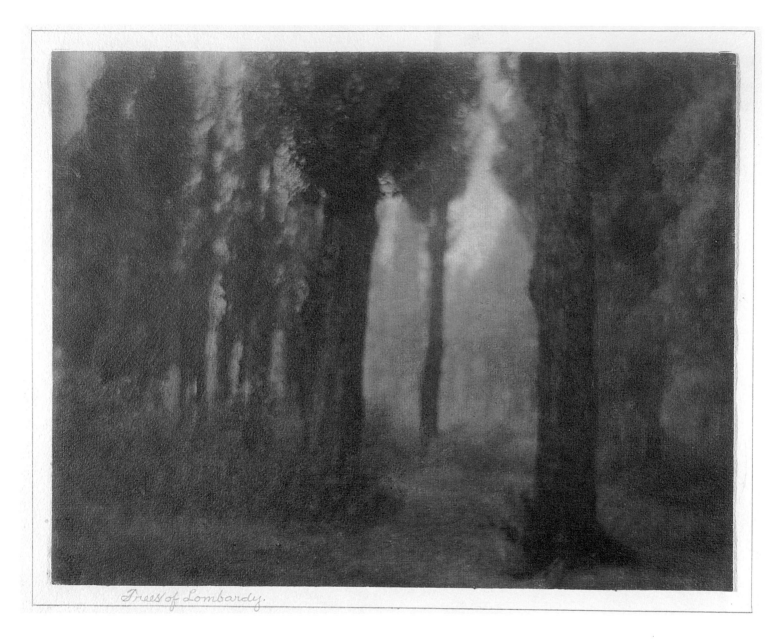

Trees of Lombardy.

WILBUR HEBER PORTERFIELD
Trees of Lombardy, 1903

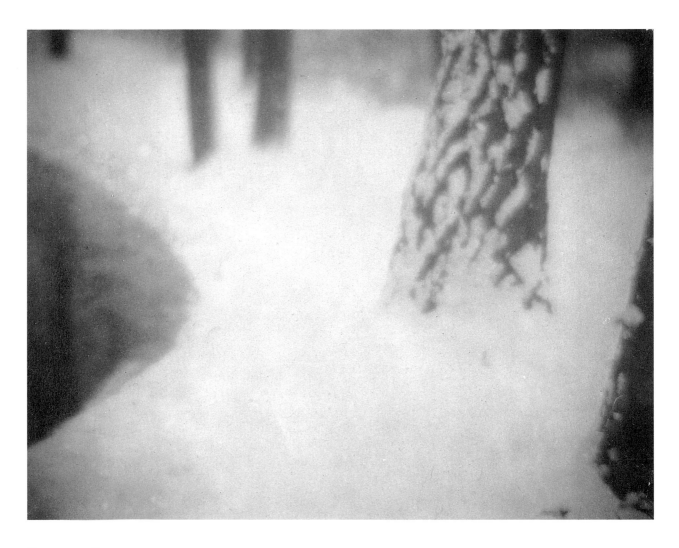

EDWARD STEICHEN
Landscape, ca. 1897

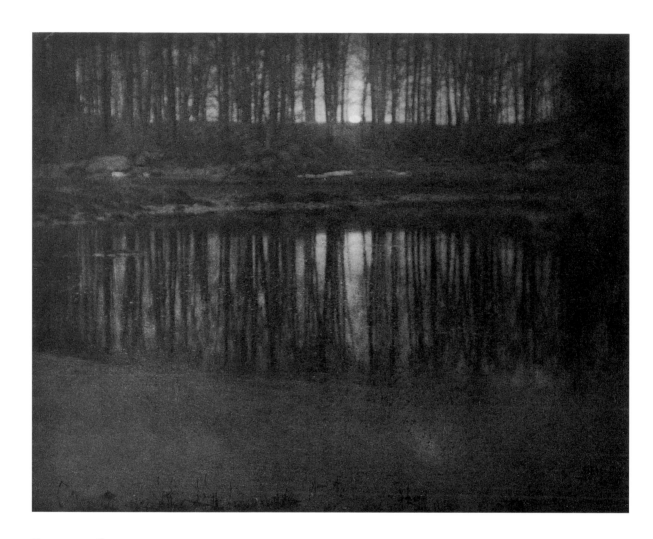

EDWARD STEICHEN
Moonlight, the Pond, 1906

ALFRED STIEGLITZ
Spring Showers, 1900 (printed ca. 1913)

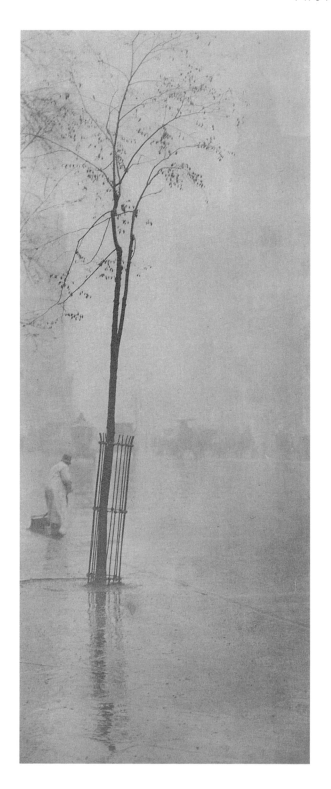

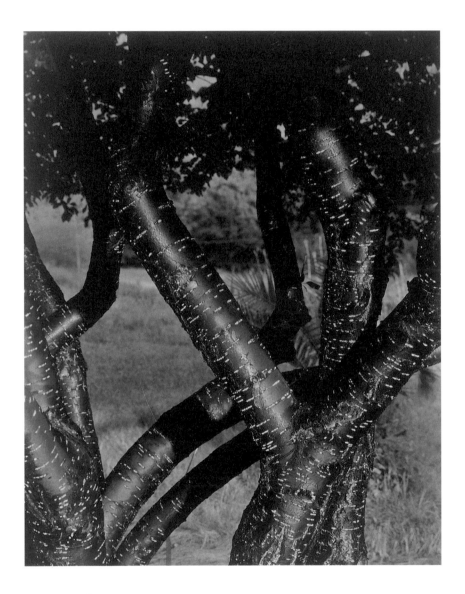

ALFRED STIEGLITZ
Dancing Trees, 1921–22

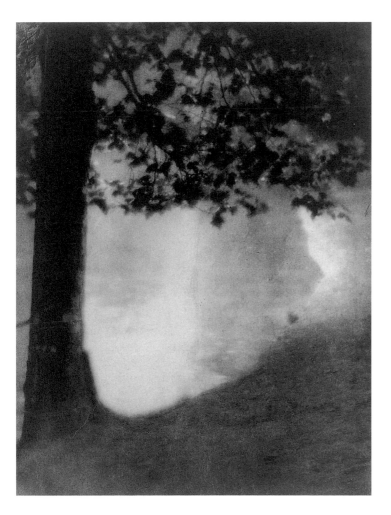

KARL STRUSS
Tree in Landscape, 1909

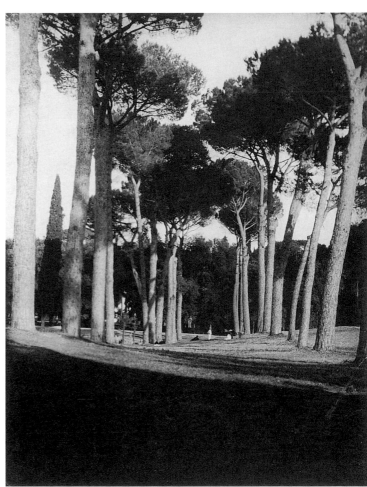

KARL STRUSS
Avenue of Pines, 1909

KARL STRUSS
In the Southland: Mt. Baldy, California, ca. 1921

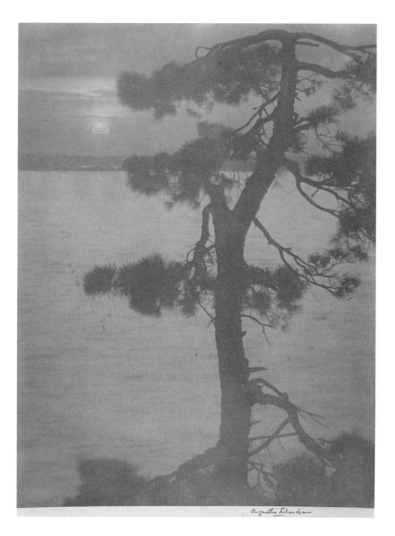

AUGUSTUS THIBAUDEAU
Lonely Pine Tree, ca. 1908

AUGUSTUS THIBAUDEAU
Lily Pad in Reflecting Pond, ca. 1910

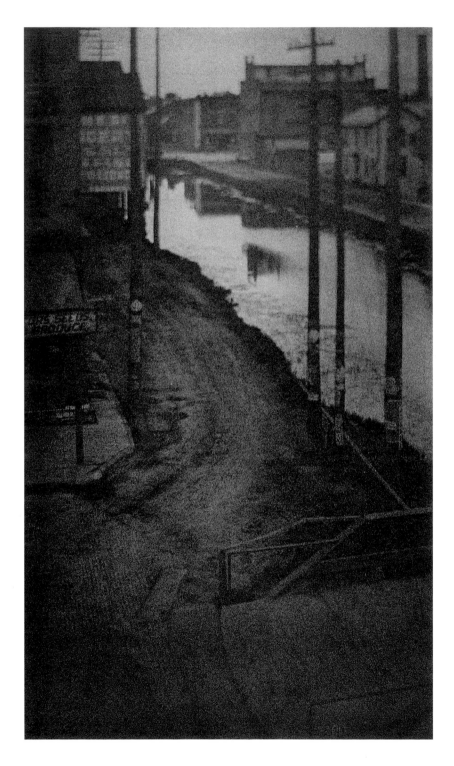

CLARENCE H. WHITE
Telegraph Poles, 1898

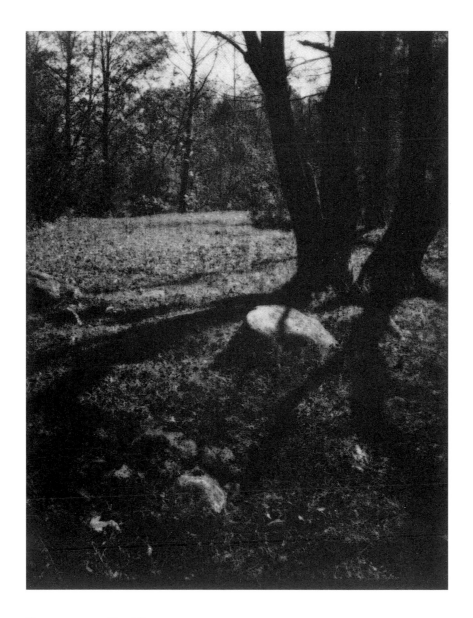

CLARENCE H. WHITE
Woodland Scene, ca. 1905

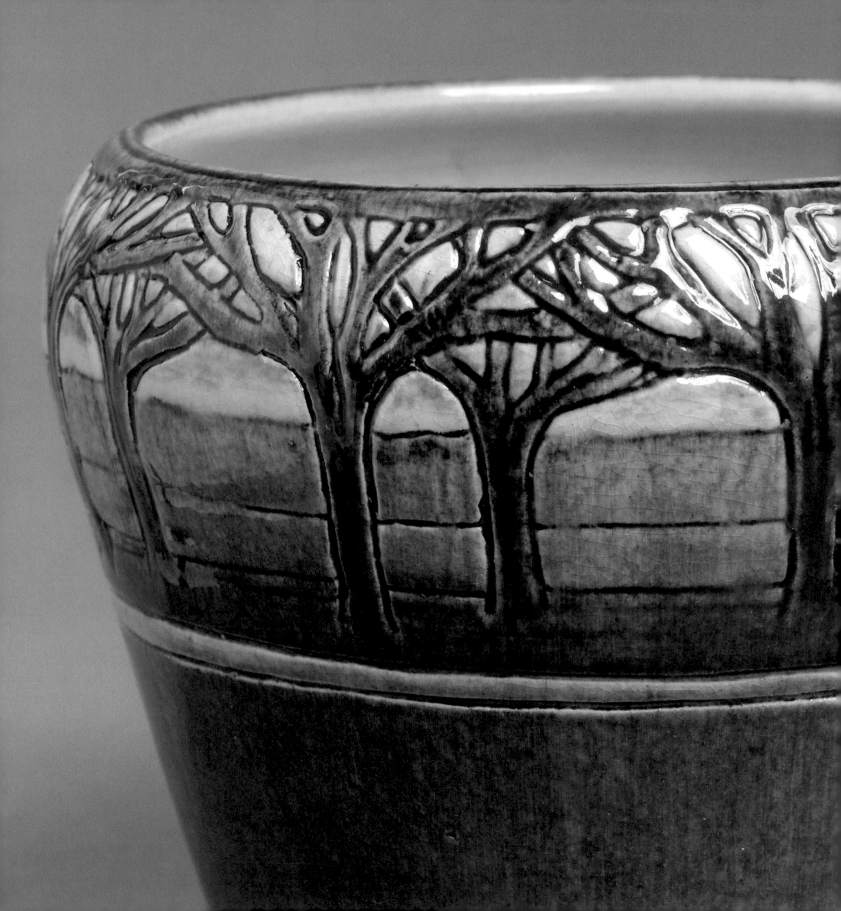

Arthur Wesley Dow and Art Pottery: The Beauty of Simplicity

by Jessie Poesch

In the early months of 1900, the lavish magazine *Keramic Studio,* the bible of the American art ceramic movement, was filled with breathless announcements about the upcoming Universal Exposition in Paris. This was to be the first major European exhibition of American hand-painted porcelains and glazed pottery. In its March issue, *Keramic Studio* published photographs of work to be sent to Paris: editor Adelaide Alsop Robineau's own plate designs, china painting by Anna B. Leonard, and specimens from the Rookwood and Grueby potteries.[1] The May issue announced that Mrs. Leonard would soon depart to study ceramic work at the South Kensington Museum in London, and then proceed to Paris; by July, Marshal Fry, critic and accomplished china painter, was in Paris.[2]

For Robineau's *Keramic Studio,* founded the previous year with the stated purpose of elevating standards of design among the many individuals engaged in the art of china painting or creating art pottery, the Paris show was a potential validation. And, indeed, when the August issue carried a list of the awards given to American ceramic exhibitors, the results were impressive. Grand prizes were bestowed on the Rookwood Company of Cincinnati and the Tiffany Glass and Decorating Company of New York. Tiffany also received

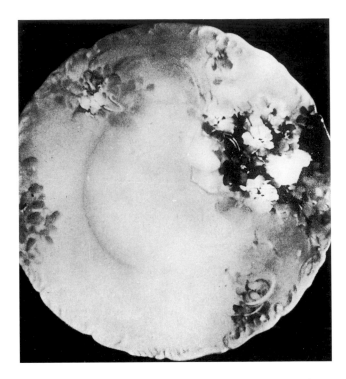

Marshal Fry, Dinner Plate Decorated with Violets. *Illustrated in* Keramic Studio 1 *(May 1899), p. 4. New York Public Library. Skillful naturalistic painting, often lush and sentimental in feeling, was much favored by china painters in the late nineteenth century. Fry created this plate before his studies with Dow.*

a gold medal for excellence as did Grueby Faience of Boston, Trenton Potteries of Trenton, New Jersey, and Maria Longworth [Nichols] Storer of Cincinnati. In addition, the judges voted bronze medals for the National League of Mineral Painters, Mrs. S. S. Frackelton of Milwaukee, the Art Department of H. Sophie Newcomb College in New Orleans, Dedham Pottery of Dedham, Massachusetts, and the Atlan Club in Chicago. In her review of the exhibition, critic Anna B. Leonard noted that many of the European designs were

surprisingly conventional, and that the American work was equal to that of the best French potters, Bigot and Delaherche. The success of the Tiffany glass and Grueby pottery made her "feel very proud," and, she said, showed that "the Schools of Design are having their influence."[3]

Meanwhile, back in the United States, two young female graduates of Newcomb College, Harriet Joor and Amelie Roman, were traveling north to attend one such design school, "the summer school of Mr. Arthur Dow in Ipswich."[4] Dow, who was widely known as a teacher and printmaker, had opened the summer school in 1891 to promote the arts and crafts aesthetic. His thought-provoking handbook *Composition: A Series of Exercises in Art Structure for the use of Students and Teachers* (1899) had been well received at the exhibition of the Society of Arts and Crafts, Boston, in April 1899, and by 1901 there were three editions and four printings. Dow's popular theories of design and composition were having a tremendous influence on the growing art ceramics movement in America.

For Harriet Joor, Ipswich was "ideal, charming from beginning to end, . . . a perfect setting in which to work and study." And she found Dow to be an inspiring teacher; her account gives a vivid insight into the nature of his program:

There were ninety students in all—art teachers, directors and ambitious aspirants—almost all of them women . . . The work was in two divisions—landscape, watercolors and charcoal, and composition and designing, the last being the more important of the two. Two days of the week were given to criticism, and the rest to problems in designing and drawing wild flowers . . . Mr. Dow took the entire class to Boston to the Art Museum and Library, and every week he would give us a lantern lecture, and we would follow him over the old world and learn at the feet of the old masters. Mr. Dow . . . carrying us with him in rare sympathy by his fine enthusiasm and personal magnetism that is so necessary in a teacher. I cannot tell you how happy we all were in the learning. I don't think there was one who did not come away feeling that his or her feet had been started on the true road to that world beautiful toward which we were all plodding, not one but loved Beauty more joyously and sincerely and had eyes and heart more reverently opened to receive it.[5]

For those who attended Dow's summer school, the experience and contacts were often the first stepping stones on the way to careers in art and teaching. A remarkable network, based on journals, books, exhibitions, special classes and courses, and apparent personal contacts existed among those involved in china painting and art pottery, as well as among others in the arts and crafts movement.

Exactly what Dow taught in his classes at the Ipswich Summer School of Art is made clearer from a series of six lectures he delivered to the New York Society of Keramic Arts in the spring of 1901. These lessons were subsequently published in *Keramic Studio,* accompanied by illustrations of ceramic work by Marshal Fry, Adelaide Alsop Robineau, Maud Mason, and others.[6] Although only one of the lessons explicitly addressed china painting, the editor noted,

"the general principles of art were demonstrated so clearly that few can fail to profit by them in designing and executing their fall work." The first two lessons covered Dow's basic concepts of form—line, color, and *notan,* or shading of dark and light. Students were given specific

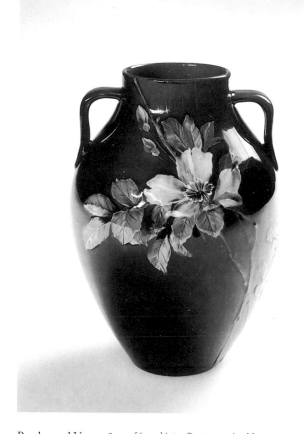

Rookwood Vase, *1891, 5⅝ × 4¼ in. Cincinnati Art Museum; gift of Walter E. Schott, Margaret C. Schott, Charles M. Williams, and Lawrence H. Kyte (1952.282). Typical of Rookwood decoration ca. 1890–95 with single-flower motifs, this example is similar to pieces that would have been familiar to Mary Given Sheerer before she joined the Newcomb College faculty.*

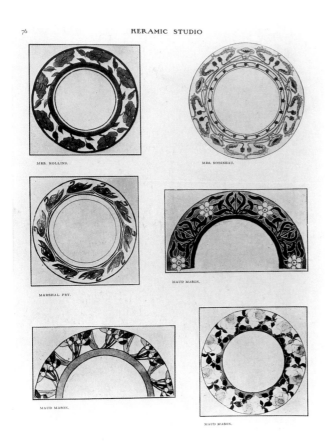

Border designs produced by Dow's class at the New York Society of Keramic Arts, in the spring of 1901. Illustration for Elizabeth Mason, "A Class in Design, Mr. Arthur Dow, Instructor," Keramic Studio 3 (August 1901), p. 76. New York Public Library

space-filling problems, such as drawing a design of tulips in a rectangular or circular space. The third lesson was an exercise in border design: "To construct a repeating border for a ten-inch plate, taking the Chelsea or Dedham plate for a model, the original having a border one and a half inches from edge, then a one-half inch smaller border and a line within that."[7]

Another lesson was devoted to Dow's principle of subordination. Students were asked "to fill a rectangular form with a center and border, . . . the border to be subordinate to the center or vice versa, according to which was designed to be the most important." The subject of the fifth session was tonal distinctions, and the final lecture was again on border designs.

The designs created under Dow's tutelage were simplified or conventionalized. In itself, this was not new to decorators of his era. Artists such as Robineau and Mary Given Sheerer, supervisor of design at Newcomb Pottery, were long familiar with the abstraction of natural forms. But Dow emphasized the relationship of the design to the space occupied. His attention to clearly defined lines, tonal differences, and the use of flat color, along with his self-conscious stress on balance and subordination, made for greater clarity, simplification, and calm. Dow's influence, though, seems to have been equal parts theory and personality. Many students reported an almost spiritual aspect to his character, a quality more easily felt than described in words. And, as a teacher, he seems to have emphasized this aura by showing original works of art whenever possible. The dramatic effect of this technique is clear in the description of his last lecture: "Dr. Dow dwelt at length upon some pieces of Corean [*sic*] pottery . . . sometimes with the mark of the potter's thumb . . . He considered that the charm of these little jars lay in their irregularity and uniqueness, the personality and freedom of the artist who fashioned them showing in every line and feature . . . he remarked on the desirability of studying from the objects themselves, as even the best colored reproductions in books are imperfect."

Dow was familiar with Korean pottery. In 1893 he served as assistant to Ernest F. Fenollosa, curator of Japanese art at the Museum of Fine Arts, Boston. This was shortly after the museum acquired the pioneer Morse collection of more than five thousand pieces of Japanese and Korean earthenware, stoneware, and porcelain.[8] (It is fair to say that familiarity with this remarkable collection also helped to shape design concepts of ceramists in the Boston milieu—those associated with Dedham, Grueby, and, later, the Marblehead and Paul Revere potteries.)

In the last lecture he gave to his New York class, Dow said that the goal of the arts and crafts movement was "to bring every one into a mental attitude wherein one picks out only the beautiful and ignores the bad." The *Keramic Studio* article summarized the lecture this way: "The great thing to learn is the beauty of simplicity, and the avoidance of the *common-place,* and what Mr. Dow terms the *wicked,* by which we conceive him to mean all violent colors, all *lying* exaggerations, both of color and form, but the wickedest of all is the *common-place.*" Marshal Fry, who was among the members of Dow's class, spoke for many art ceramists when he observed, "Mr. Dow has done much toward opening a way for us to gain that which we need . . . [we decorators have] mistaken our ceramic forms for nothing more than surfaces upon which to represent flowers and figures, instead of first of all studying form, and to a beautiful form adding only such decoration as

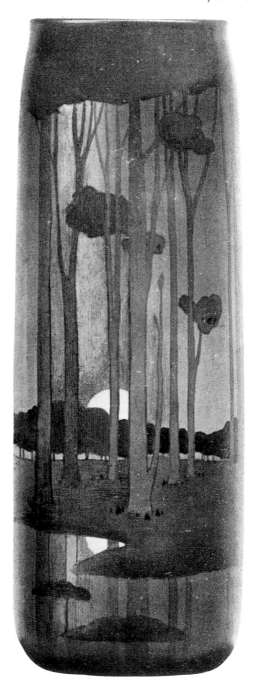

Vase painted by Marshal Fry after his study with Dow. Illustrated in Keramic Studio *5 (February 1904), p. 222. New York Public Library*

would be carrying further, an enhancing of the form itself."[9]

The extent to which Fry's own overglaze decoration was transformed by his study with Dow is made clear by four examples of his work later illustrated in *Keramic Studio.* On a tall vase, a romantic image of a grove of trees with a moon rising over a low horizon at the base is related directly to the form of the vase (p. 113). The effect of the clearly defined linear imagery was enhanced by the colors. "Such a keen and delicate understanding of the subtleties of color harmony . . . places [Fry's] work on a par with the best painting in any medium," noted one contemporary critic. "There was a mystery and fullness of color in its purple greens that showed a deep appreciation of the poetry of nature."[10]

When Joor and Roman returned to Newcomb College that fall, the design principles they had learned from Dow immediately transformed the work at Newcomb Pottery. Newcomb Pottery had been initiated in 1895 to provide a model handicrafts industry for young women trained in the decorative arts but unable to find work. Though based in part on the successful Rookwood Pottery in Cincinnati, Newcomb Pottery sought to distinguish itself from Rookwood in several ways. Green, blue, yellow, and black were chosen as the basic colors; shapes were traditional; no two pieces were alike; and the designs were based on the flora and fauna of the Gulf Coast, "the blue flag, the yellow jasmine, the tiger lily; the forests of pine, magnolia and cypress." When possible, local clays were used to try to create a "genuinely local product."[11] Designs were repeated around

the piece, so that a vase, for example, could be viewed equally from any vantage point. As a further distancing from Rookwood products, the images on the early Newcomb pieces were painted on the biscuit and given a glossy glaze. But Newcomb Pottery never attained the technical virtuosity of Rookwood.

In 1901 Harriet Joor created an encircling, boldly incised design in blues and grays on a tyg, or three-handled drinking mug (p. 137). This is possibly the earliest example of a Newcomb piece in which the design was incised directly onto the leather-hard surface of the clay rather than, as earlier, painted on the biscuit. The design itself represents an almost direct translation of the space-filling problem given in the chapter titled "Line, Landscape Composition" in Dow's book *Composition.* There Dow stated, "The picture, the plan, and the pattern are alike in the sense that each is a group of synthetically related spaces." For example, Dow wrote, "Looking out from a grove we notice that the trees, vertical straight lines, cut horizontal lines—an arrangement in opposition and repetition making a pattern in rectangular spaces."[12] In Joor's piece, there is a subtle suggestion of depth, giving it a slight painterly quality. This might be called the "grove of trees" problem (see p. 115): Only a section of the grove is depicted, thus stressing the contrast between the vertical lines and the horizontal framework. A horizontal wall hanging from Newcomb embroidered in autumnal browns, greens, and oranges shows another spatial composition of the same theme (p. 197).

Dow's teaching methods at Ipswich were

increasingly innovative. By 1902, when china painter Elizabeth Mason attended the school, Dow was interested in a range of crafts: students produced brass candle shades, baskets, stencils, and weaving. Pottery was made "from clay which they themselves had dug from the brooks . . . [and] fired in a little kiln which Mr. Dow had near his studio on 'Bayberry Hill.'"[13] In 1903 Dow's continuing studies of different cultures (which led to his acquaintance with ethnologist Frank Hamilton Cushing, who had lived with the Zuni in the American West) prompted him to emphasize "primitive handicrafts" made from the simplest materials. As exercises in design, Dow encouraged his pupils at Ipswich "to look to the common things around them for carrying out their work—the barks, the roots, the fibers, the reeds, the rushes, the plants, the sticks, stones, clays and sands. The capabilities of these things in diverse directions are studied, and in this way much is learned about the technical and artistic possibilities and the natural limitations of the objects the pupils set out to make."[14]

When writer Sylvester Baxter visited the school in the summer of 1903, he noted Dow's view of the handicraft-versus-machine debate that then divided the arts and crafts movement: "Just as there is no special virtue inherent in a thing because it is common and domestic, so there is no special merit in handicraft in and of itself . . . Properly viewed, the machine is an industrial emancipator. It lightens work and makes its products plentiful and cheap." The virtue for artists and designers of using a hand-loom, for example, was that it was "educative, disciplinary, directing

represent nature's forms, colors and effects; must know the properties of pigments and how to handle brushes and materials. He may have to study the sciences of perspective and anatomy. More or less of this knowledge and skill will be required in his career, but they are only helps to art, not substitutes for it, and I believe that if he begins with Composition, that is, with a study of art itself, he will acquire these naturally, as he feels the need of them.

Returning now to the thought that the picture and the abstract design are much alike in structure, let us see how some of the simple spacings may be illustrated by landscape.

Looking out from a grove we notice that the trees, vertical straight lines, cut horizontal lines,—an arrangement in Opposition and Repetition making a pattern in rectangular spaces. Compare the gingham and landscape on page 22. This is a common effect in nature, to be translated into terms of art as suggested in the following exercise.

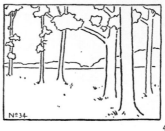

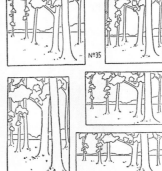

EXERCISE

No. 34 is a landscape reduced to its main lines, all detail being omitted.

Make an enlarged copy of this, or design a similar one. Then, in the attempt to find the best proportion and the best way of setting the subject upon canvas or paper, arrange this in rectangles of varying shape, some nearly square, others tall, others long and narrow horizontally as in No. 35. To bring the whole landscape into all these will not, of course, be possible, but in each the essential lines must be retained.

Draw in ink after preliminary studies with pencil or charcoal, correcting errors by tracing.

Then find in nature other similar subjects; sketch and vary in the same way.

45

The "grove of trees problem." "Landscape reduced to its main lines, all details omitted," with five alternate examples in different proportions— arrangements in opposition and repetitions. From Arthur Wesley Dow, Composition *(New York, 1913), p. 45. Howard-Tilton Memorial Library, Tulane University, New Orleans*

the attention to proper beginnings and making training in industry more fundamental, more radical in its quality; first going to the root of things, and thence reaching higher ends." These attitudes, as Baxter recognized, expressed the optimism of a utopian reformer: "By thus giving to the machine its due recognition, it is conceivable that the arts and crafts at Ipswich might become a powerful factor in the new industrial

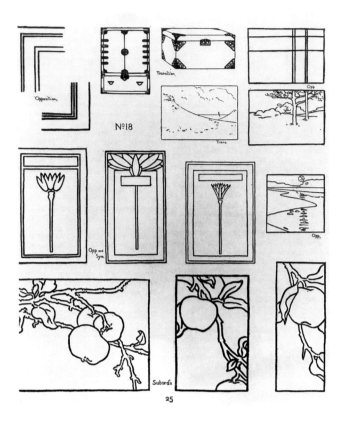

"Principles of Composition III." From Arthur Wesley Dow, Composition *(New York, 1913), p. 25. Howard-Tilton Memorial Library, Tulane University, New Orleans. Dow's examples of exercises or problems in the analysis and arrangement of lines within differently shaped spaces.*

dispensation that must dawn for the world as our civilization seeks an equilibrium upon the new level established by the era of mechanical production and distribution. With his artistic, social, and economic ideals, Mr. Dow is well fitted to take an important part in such a movement."[15]

Meanwhile, Dow's ideas of design continued to have a strong influence on the designs of New-comb Pottery until around 1910.[16] In reviewing

the development of designs on Newcomb pottery up to 1910, Mary Given Sheerer told a writer that when the students came to the pottery "they met the problem of learning to design on round surfaces, and with respect to the limitations of the material used."[17] A good example of Newcomb work is a cream-colored vase designed by Roberta Kennon around 1903 (p. 139), on which bold incised lines outline leaves that spread out to fit the shape of the vessel forming a border at the neck and shoulder. A bowl in muted tones made by Marie Levering Benson in 1907 (p. 147) has a soft, blue-grey background and a decorative tree motif in a slightly brighter blue. Narrow at the base and wider at the top, the spreading con-figuration of the leaves (done in incised lines as if they were little kernels) appropriately fits the shape.

Gertrude Roberts Smith had taught design at Newcomb College before Sheerer's arrival, and continued to do so. In 1902 she had initiated a program in artistic embroidery and needlework, and had collected various examples of hand-loom weaving and handwoven baskets.[18] The large em-broidered wall hanging with the grove-of-trees motif, already mentioned, is an excellent example of work done under Smith's instruction, as is a five-foot-long table runner (p. 198), which fea-tures the motif of a tall central pine tree flanked by smaller ones and set against a muted back-ground of multicolored threads. As in virtually all known examples of Newcomb embroidery, these pieces feature fairly simple stitches—satin and outline, darning and buttonhole. Colored threads of Persian silks were applied to heavy linens, or in some cases, to cottons. There is an example of a table runner (Louisiana State University Museum of Art) designed by Pauline Wright Nichols for which the original outline sketch of a design and the template used to cut the major masses or silhouette have survived.[19] This demonstrates the design process apparently used by many of these needlework artists: first, an outline sketch of the design was made, then a template was cut of the major masses or silhouettes. This outline was then transferred to the fabric and the flat areas of color were filled with embroidery stitches.

After the Ipswich summer session of 1903, Dow, his wife, and his brother Dana departed on a year-long journey around the world. They spent three full months in Japan, touring the obvious sights, ancient temples, and gardens. They visited many artists and art schools, and purchased a large number of prints and printing equipment, such as cut woodblocks. Dow also revealed a hands-on interest in ceramics. On November 2 he visited the Higher Technical School and its Higher Normal School near Tokyo. He found the drawing and design classes disappointing, but was enthralled by the pottery, where "the most interesting thing was the turning by hand—an old man was at work with a wheel which he whirled by means of a stick inserted in a hollow in its upper [?] surface." Dow made a drawing of this and watched while the craftsman turned some vases and cups. In another room, he observed how plates were being made by machine. He sketched the particular kind of iron knife being used to press the clay, which was

then "slapped upon a plaster mould on another wheel." He made notes and another drawing in which he diagramed how he thought the drafts in the kilns worked.[20]

On November 7 the party visited Makojima and discovered another pottery in the "Garden of the 100 flowers." Dow seems instantly to have established a rapport with the potter who was "painting on the ware." Dow noted in his diary, "He had bowls of black, red, green and white. He painted on the biscuit, then coated it with a white glaze put on with a big, flat brush. I painted an Ipswich marsh haystack as he invited me to try . . . He also put our names on some saucers. They were fired within an hour!" He made drawings of two different kilns. Pine wood was used for firing, "there was no chimney and I cannot find [?] how the draft is made. But the whole interior was red hot."[21]

Upon his return to America, Dow was invited to direct the Department of Fine Arts at Teachers College Columbia University. There, he completely reorganized the department, recruiting many former students and colleagues for the faculty. His own course, which he liked to call "art structure," focused on the theory and practice of teaching art. Other faculty members taught more specialized subjects. By 1911–12 the department offered fourteen different courses; a decade later, there were thirty. In 1909 Dow published his second book, *Theory and Practice of Teaching Art*.[22] As in *Composition*, in this manual Dow melded Japanese and Western ideas.[23] The problems presented, though primarily relevant to a variety of craftsmen and designers, were also applicable to painters of landscape and still life. The work of two of Dow's most famous pupils, painters Max Weber and Georgia O'Keeffe, demonstrates his influence.

Still another example of Dow's role in shaping American art pottery is the story of his impact on the famous Overbeck sisters. Even before they founded their own pottery, the four Overbeck sisters held a place of high esteem in the world of American ceramics. Between May 1901 and March 1913, seventeen different issues of *Keramic Studio* included one or more designs for china painting by Margaret Overbeck. Between 1904 and 1916, forty-seven issues carried designs by her sister, Hannah, seven years younger. And between 1904 and 1916 twenty-two issues carried one or more designs by their youngest sister, Mary Frances.[24] Theirs was a high level of creative activity.[25]

In 1904 or 1905 Margaret Overbeck studied design with Dow at Columbia, at a time when Marshal Fry also taught there.[26] But even then she was already internationally known for her designs for china painting. In 1901 she had won a prize for plate design from *Keramic Studio,* in a contest judged by Dow. And in March 1907 Robineau devoted virtually the entire issue of *Keramic Studio* to designs and texts by Margaret Overbeck. A handsome full-page color supplement featured a landscape in rich russets, blues, and reds, a scene very much in the Dow woodblock idiom. Five drawings illustrated how this landscape design could be adapted to a bowl, a vase, and to tiles for low and high ferneries or palmstands. Twenty-eight other illustrations offered designs for plates, cups and saucers, and borders.

The texts by Margaret Overbeck apply Dow's principles to the design of ceramics:

> Consider first the piece and its use. Avoid over-ornate decoration on all pieces in the service used for meats, vegetables, etc. . . . strange to say many a one, in painting a set of plates, will want them to look more like "hand painting," which may mean a spreading cluster of some favorite flower, never suspecting that if a plate has a decoration that is so strikingly real it is everlastingly unfitted for contact with a meat course, unless a generous treatment of hydrofluoric acid is administered . . . the shapes in both background and unit of design must be related, not only to each other, but to the space occupied, that there may be balance and rhythm in the whole.[27]

Margaret Overbeck is rightfully seen as the catalyst behind the formation of the Overbeck Pottery. She trained Hannah and Mary Frances in china painting, and she no doubt helped to set the two principal standards for the pottery—that all pieces must be completely handcrafted and that no two pieces should be alike. Margaret died suddenly in 1911 as a result of an automobile accident, but that year the other three sisters carried out her dream and established a small pottery at their home in Cambridge, Indiana—a business that continued until 1955. The most creative period was 1911 to 1936; for the last nineteen years, Mary Frances carried on alone.

Hannah Overbeck attended the Indiana State Normal School (now Indiana State University) in Terre Haute in 1894, and then taught for a year in Clinton, Indiana. But because of ill health, she returned home. In the last six years of her life, she had chronic neuritis and could no longer draw. But her design of repeated hummingbirds for fireplace tiles, made of sharp, geometric angles, suggests the strength and originality of her work and is a portent of some of the sharply angular forms used later in Overbeck Pottery.

Mary Frances Overbeck, the youngest of the sisters involved in ceramics, also attended the Indiana State Normal School. She then taught for a time in Boulder, Colorado, and at some point studied with Dow at Columbia. She was thirty-three years old when the sisters began the pottery in 1911.[28] Mary Frances was skilled as a painter and designer, and her bookplate designs became well known. Elizabeth Overbeck, the middle sister, did not go away to study until 1909. According to an article written by Mary in 1944, Elizabeth "was housekeeper for her parents as long as they lived. After they died, she took a course in ceramics under Charles Fergus Binns at the New York State School of Clayworking and Ceramics at Alfred University, New York." Though the parents died in 1904 and 1906, Elizabeth did not take the course at Alfred until 1909, so she must have been responsible for housekeeping for a good while. She was thirty-six when the pottery began.[29] Elizabeth's training as a ceramic technician was the lynchpin that made the pottery project possible. She made the clay mixtures, developed the glaze recipes, and turned the pieces on the wheel.

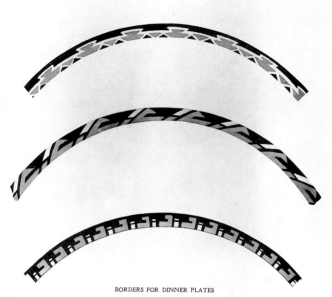

BORDERS FOR DINNER PLATES

TWO shades of green, blue, red, or brown—all more or less subdued—and gold for black parts would be an effective treatment for these simple designs. In any case the color in the largest masses should be most subdued, depending for richness upon the gold background, and purer color in the smaller forms.

Margaret Overbeck, Border Designs for Dinner Plates. Illustrated in Keramic Studio 8 (March 1907), p. 252. Howard-Tilton Memorial Library, Tulane University, New Orleans

From 1911 to 1931 the three surviving sisters— Hannah, Mary Frances, and Elizabeth—appear to have worked very closely together. Hannah and Mary Frances worked interchangeably as designer-decorators. On those pieces for which Hannah was the major decorator, there is an "H" alongside the mark of the Overbeck Pottery; those primarily created by Mary Frances bear an "F" (thus not usurping what would have been the "M" for Margaret). During this period, the reputation of the Overbeck Pottery grew slowly but steadily. "It was slow work, as the Pottery could afford little advertising," Mary later recalled.

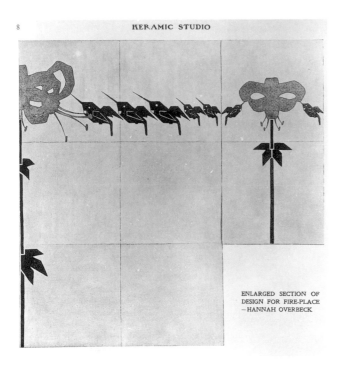

Hannah Overbeck, Section of a Fireplace Design. *From Keramic Studio 8 (December 1900), p. 178. Howard-Tilton Memorial Library, Tulane University, New Orleans*

"The Pottery became known mostly by one person telling another person about it."[30] They supplemented their income by teaching classes in design in their basement workshop or in nearby Richmond. The bowls, vases, and occasional commissioned pieces are among their most distinguished wares.[31]

In their early works, the Overbecks often favored matte glazes with flowing incised designs of plants—but in subdued colors. The large leaves of a hosta plant in green, against a cream background, form a repeat motif on a tall, elegant vase, the outlines done in firmly incised lines (p. 153). Some vases are monochromatic with intricate, somewhat abstracted carved patterns. There is an almost staccato rhythm to the geometric designs on some of the later pieces; the colors are bright and the glazes are glossy. Some of these were created in the 1920s and 1930s. They are by no means slick Art Deco designs, yet they do have some of the jagged rhythmic aspects of products of that era, though with greater intricacy and subtlety. In several works, the complex overall pattern features flat linear figures and shapes. The intricate angular patterning is related to that on pre-Columbian pots from Central America but is in no way derivative; the sharp-edged angularity was already seen in Hannah's designs of 1906.[32]

Technically, the products of the Overbeck Pottery are varied and sometimes complex. Vessels were made of earthenware and porcelain. Designs were often first worked out on paper, then incised into or carved out of the surface. In some cases, fine clay inlays were used; after the design was incised on the surface, a second clay was pressed into the excavation.[33] The designs feature birds, animals, and sometimes fantasylike circles for treetops, and the images sometimes overlap.

In the years following the Universal Exposition of 1900, in Paris, arts and crafts societies proliferated in the United States. A succession of local and national exhibitions provided ceramists with key opportunities to show their wares. Of the larger international fairs, the Louisiana Purchase Exposition in Saint Louis in 1904 provided the most important showcase for arts and crafts exhibitors. Frederic Allen Whiting, the secretary and treasurer of the Society of Arts and Crafts in Boston, reviewed the craft work shown in Saint Louis for *International Studio,* noting that the potter's craft was "more largely represented than any other."[34] Whiting spoke favorably of Dedham's crackleware with blue decoration, Grueby, Newcomb, and Charles Volkmar, as well as the Merrimac Pottery, Teco, Van Briggle, and Rookwood. Pieces by Marshal Fry, Adelaide Alsop Robineau, "pupils of the State School of Clayworking and Ceramics, at Alfred," and Miss McLaughlin of Cincinnati were among those mentioned. Characteristic of much of the new ceramic work was a tendency toward what Whiting called "formalized nature." "One of the chief influences in this wholesome progress," Whiting reported, "is that of Mr. A. W. Dow, the general principles of whose teaching are not, however, restricted to apply exclusively to keramics or to any one particular branch of art." Marshal Fry and Anna Leonard, both of whom were teaching special classes, were identified as disciples of Dow, as were the Misses Mason.

Whiting gave considerable credit to the editors of *Keramic Studio* for their yeoman's service in fostering a "revival of serious interest in keramics," an aspect of decorative arts that Whiting noted "was recently but a weedy field of native art."

For its part, *Keramic Studio* responded by publishing an extensive series of articles (from January through May of 1905) detailing the ceramics shown in Saint Louis. In particular, the journal noted the large number of potteries that had sprung into existence "like mushrooms after the rain."[35] Among the relative newcomers ex-

hibiting at Saint Louis were Arthur E. Baggs, Frederick Walrath, and Charles Fergus Binns (all listed as from the New York State School of Clayworking and Ceramics at Alfred University, in Alfred, New York), as well as Addison B. LeBoutillier of Grueby Faience Company.[36]

In fact, Walrath and Baggs can be identified as part of a second wave of art potteries, partly influenced by Binns. Trained as a ceramic scientist at the Royal Worcester Porcelain Works, Binns had come to the United States in 1893, the year of the Chicago World's Fair. In 1900 he became director of the newly established New York State School of Clayworking and Ceramics at Alfred University and soon established it as a major center for the study of ceramic technology.[37] While sympathetic to china painters and pottery decorators, he advocated professional knowledge and involvement with the entire process of creation, from clay preparation to final firing, and he was known for his matte glazes. Binns soon became an important force in the ceramics world, both as a teacher and as a frequent writer in magazines such as *Keramic Studio* and *The Craftsman.*[38] His book *The Manual of Practical Pottery* was in its third edition by 1901.[39]

Walrath studied with Binns at Alfred University in 1902–03, then taught his own course at the Rochester Athenaeum and Mechanics Institute. He established his own pottery firm in Rochester, making vases in traditional shapes with matte glazes and softly muted tones. There are greens, blues, beiges, and touches of warm reds or pinks. The designs, in flat areas or patterns of color, are within clearly defined geometric areas. The whole creates an effect of austere and quiet dignity, a feeling associated with Dow's precepts. In the fall of 1918, Walrath replaced Paul Cox as ceramist at Newcomb Pottery. Unfortunately, his health was poor, and he died in September 1921.[40]

Baggs created ceramics with much the same mood as Walrath's, and with somewhat similar soft matte glazes.[41] His firm, Marblehead Pottery in Massachusetts, had its beginnings as part of a group of art industries, known as the Handicraft Shops, where weaving, wood-carving, and metalwork were taught to convalescents. But the technical requirements of the pottery were too exacting for outpatients, so, by 1906, it was set up as a separate endeavor. After studying with Binns at Alfred, Baggs took a vacation job at Marblehead, setting up equipment and making initial experiments. It was not until 1908, however, that Marblehead Pottery made its "bow to the public." By then, there was a staff of six, including Hanna Tutt as the chief decorator.[42] Some of the Marblehead vases with matte glazes and painted underglaze decoration are even more austere than Walrath's. There are often evenly divided spaces around a vase and simple geometric motifs near the neck; some have incised lines, others are painted in flat colors. On several, there are scenic views of the marshes near Marblehead, depicted in flat areas of color suggestive of Dow's block prints. Neither Baggs nor Tutt have been directly identified with Dow, though by this time his principles were well known in the Boston milieu.

Paul Cox, another Binns student from Alfred, joined the faculty at Newcomb in 1910 as a ce-

ramic chemist. He introduced a blue matte glaze, replacing the early glossy glazes, and favored a higher level of production. Rather than "straight line" designs, Cox emphasized more naturalistic designs carved in low relief. Cox seems to have dominated the design process from 1910 until 1918, while Mary Sheerer focused more on teaching the undergraduate students.

By 1918 profound changes had taken place at Newcomb and elsewhere. The arts and crafts movement had waned, and automobiles, war, radios, and voting rights for women were reshaping society. At Newcomb College, the young women who were graduating were finding new opportunities to work in the arts, particularly after World War I. During the twenty-three-year period between 1895 and 1918, eighty-three women were employed full or part time at the Newcomb Pottery; in the twenty-two-year period between 1918 and 1940, only thirty-seven women were so employed, and six of these had been with the pottery before 1918.[43]

One of the implicit aims of the arts and crafts movement, and of Dow as a teacher, was to train the artist-craftsmen who would be involved in the entire process of material production. In the history of the art potteries, this was seldom true. In 1910 Mary Sheerer at Newcomb told a reporter, "It has been the desire of all concerned that the decorator should also form the base, glaze and fire it, which would be in keeping with the best tenets of art; but this would have consumed so much time that hitherto it has not been attempted."[44] Adelaide Alsop Robineau achieved the status of an individual studio potter. Grueby,

Dedham, and Marblehead were small operations and within each there was some division of labor. Though the responsibilities of the three Overbeck sisters were different, they seem to have worked so closely together in deciding upon design, shape, decoration, and glazes that they were indeed effectively a "studio pottery," a prototype for many later twentieth-century ceramists. In each of these art potteries, however, it is fair to say that the designers and decorators were familiar with the entire pottery process. They knew something of the problems and hazards of different types of clay, often shared or even designed the shapes, were frequently involved in the application of glazes, and, with their colleagues, were responsible for the design.

Dow was not himself a ceramist, but he was familiar with the processes involved, knew about the history of ceramic design, and welcomed ceramic designers as his students. He was a teacher, and he was a teacher of teachers. His books became handbooks. His warm personality and obvious care for his subject in the classroom motivated dozens of students to follow in his footsteps. He presented not only his core ideas about design but also showed examples of works of art from many different cultures: Japanese prints, Gothic sculpture, Venetian lace, Peruvian textiles, Greek vases and sculpture, Renaissance paintings, Persian woolens, Rembrandt drawings, Spanish architecture, and medieval metalwork.

As art historian Nancy Green argues in this publication, there were interwoven associations between Dow and the leading printmakers and photographers of his day. By the same token,

there was a network among Dow and the ceramists he taught. Harriet Joor, Amelie Roman, and Maude Robinson each became teachers. Marshal Fry and Adelaide Alsop Robineau later taught their own classes. Fry taught with Dow at Columbia and with Binns at Alfred University. Walrath took courses with Binns and, in turn, taught at the Rochester Athenaeum and Mechanics Institute and Newcomb. Dow's influence on ceramic art was strongest in the years preceding World War I, a period that coincided with the years the arts and crafts movement flourished. Influencing a generation of students, Dow's concepts were pondered from the East Coast to the West. In his effort to synthesize and find principles underlying the art of East and West, of craft and industry, of ancient and modern, Dow served as a catalyst, stimulating designers, ceramists, and art potteries. They, in turn, created their own styles and idioms, American styles characterized by restraint and sobriety.

Dow's concepts of design had a direct impact on the ceramic designs of the Newcomb, Marblehead, Walrath, Paul Revere, and Overbeck potteries— all potteries in which the design of surface embellishment was an integral part of the total effect. China painters who studied with him and were influenced by his ideas include Adelaide Alsop Robineau, Marshal Fry, Maud Mason, and Margaret and Mary Frances Overbeck. One can sense Dow's influence in some of the products of the Rookwood, Dedham, Grueby, Volkmar, and Paul Revere potteries, and Batchelder tiles, and upon still others.

NOTES

1. "Paris Exhibit, Anna B. Leonard"; "Paris Exhibit, Adelaide Alsop Robineau"; "Rookwood Pottery for Paris Exposition"; and C. Howard Walker, "The Grueby Pottery," *Keramic Studio* 1 (March 1900): 220, 231, 237.

2. *Keramic Studio* 2 (May 1900); 1 (July 1900): 62.

3. Anna B. Leonard, "Pottery and Porcelain at the Paris Exposition," *Keramic Studio* 2 (August 1900): 73–75.

4. New Orleans *Times-Democrat*, May 14, 1900, and June 17, 1900. Both were designers for Newcomb Pottery; Jessie Poesch, *Newcomb Pottery: An Enterprise for Southern Women 1895–1940* (West Chester, Pa.: Schiffer Publishing Ltd., 1984), pp. 27–28.

5. Unidentified newspaper clipping, date not clear. Josephine Louise Newcomb's scrapbook, Tulane University Archives, p. 65.

6. Elizabeth Mason, "A Class in Design, Mr. Arthur Dow, Instructor," *Keramic Studio* 5 (August 1903): 75–80.

7. As in most how-to articles in *Keramic Studio,* the comments and directions were specific. "An irregular border necessarily gives somewhat more motion than a symmetrical one, so any forms which have the effect of slanting too much from left to right or vice versa, must be avoided . . . A good way to do [it] is to draw your design roughly, fill in with flat color and hold at a distance to get the effect of the *spots.* If this general effect is restful the design will most likely be a success." Ibid.

8. Arthur Warren Johnson, *Arthur Wesley Dow, Historian, Artist, Teacher* (Ipswich, Mass.: Ipswich Historical Society 28, 1934), p. 62; Edward S. Morse, *Catalogue of the Morse Collection of Japanese Pottery* (Cambridge, Mass.: Museum of Fine Arts, 1903; new edition, Rutland, Vt.: C. E. Tuttle, 1979), intro. by Terence Barlow, pp. xii–xiv.

9. Marshal Fry, "National League," *Keramic Studio* 4 (February 1903): 214–15.

10. "The Exhibition of the New York Society of Keramic Arts," *Keramic Studio* 5 (February 1904): 222–24.

11. Nathaniel Wright Stephenson, "Newcomb College and Art in Education," *Forensic Quarterly* 1 (September 1910): 254–61.

12. Seventh ed. (New York: Doubleday, Page & Company, 1913), pp. 44–45.

13. Elizabeth Mason, "Mr. Arthur W. Dow's Summer School at Ipswich, Mass.," *Keramic Studio* 4 (October 1902): 123.

14. Sylvester Baxter, "Handicraft, and Its Extension at Ipswich," *Handicraft 1,* no. 11 (February 1903): 249–68.

15. Ibid. Given the many contradictions within the Arts and Crafts movement's critique of industry, it is no surprise that a book of essays about the art program Dow later established at Teachers College Columbia University was titled *Art and Industry in Education* (New York: Raymond V. Long, 1912).

16. Between 1902 and 1906 five more designers from Newcomb received summer scholarships to Dow's Ipswich Summer School of Art: Mary D. Bates and Roberta Kennon in 1902; Desiree Roman in 1904; Henrietta Bailey in 1905; and Marie Benson in 1906. Others also attended. Amelie Roman repeated her attendance at least three more times. Harriet Joor was there again in 1903, as was Maude Robinson, who designed pottery, practiced embroidery, and made leaded glass objects, lampshades, and fire screens. Robinson spent three summers studying with Dow, and later taught a class in ceramics in New York.

17. Stephenson, "Newcomb College," p. 259.

18. Ellsworth Woodward, "Art Needlework in Newcomb College," *The Craftsman* 5 (December 1903): 282–85. In 1901 Smith made a series of visits to other art schools, establishing contacts and gaining insights into their programs. She visited the Corcoran Art School in Washington, Drexel Institute of Art, Science, and Industry in Philadelphia, Pratt Institute in Brooklyn, and the Women's School of Applied Design in New York. Next she visited the Rhode Island School of Design, the Massachusetts Normal Art School, and Denman Ross at Harvard, "and then went over to Ipswich for some study." See "Educators' Return," New Orleans *Times-Democrat*, August 31, 1901.

19. Illustrated in James C. Jordan III et al., *Southern Arts and Crafts, 1890–1940* (Charlotte, N.C.: Mint Museum of Art, 1996), p. 73. This is one of the relatively few examples of

Newcomb embroidery in which the name of the artist is known.

20. Arthur Wesley Dow Travel Diary, 1903. Dow Papers, Roll 1209, Archives of American Art, Smithsonian Institution, Washington, D.C.

21. Ibid.

22. New York: Teachers College Columbia University, 1909.

23. Dow's interest in pottery and porcelains, as well as his practice of teaching from original objects, continued during these busy years. Among his letters is one written January 16, 1910, in which he noted, "Yesterday I spoke to teachers on Chinese Porcelain at the Metropolitan Museum." Dow to Everett [Hubbard], Dow Papers, Roll 1033, Archives of American Art, Smithsonian Institution, Washington, D.C.

24. Often more than one of the Overbeck designs was included in a single issue. The March 1907 issue devoted nineteen pages to designs and text by Margaret; the November 1913 issue had seven pages of Hannah's work. See the list of designs by the Overbeck sisters appearing in *Keramic Studio* as given by Kathleen R. Postle, *The Chronicle of the Overbeck Pottery* (Indianapolis: Indiana Historical Society, 1978), pp. 97–100. Postle's work is the fundamental study; she knew the Overbeck sisters and had access to some of the material now lost.

25. The Overbeck sisters involved in the pottery were Margaret, Hannah, Elizabeth, and Mary Frances. There were also two other sisters, Ida, born 1861, who had a photographic studio (ca. 1890–1893) and who married in 1893; and Harriet (1872–1947), a talented musician and linguist, who, after her studies, lived with her sisters in the family home and was the housekeeper for the family; and a brother, Charles (1881–1931), who was an engineer. Lillian H. Crowley, "It's Now the Potter's Turn," *International Studio* 75 (September 1922): 539–46; *American Art Annual* 26 (1929): 728–29; 27 (1930): 556; 29 (1932): 507–08; [Mary Overbeck], "Necrology. Elizabeth Gray Overbeck," *American Ceramic Society Bulletin* 16 (February 1937): 67; [Mary Overbeck], "Overbeck Pottery," *American Ceramic Society Bulletin* 23 (May 15, 1944): 155–58.

26. Margaret Overbeck had first studied watercolor, woodcarving, and oil painting at the Art Academy of Cincinnati in 1892–93. She was there again in 1898–99. After teaching at several institutions, she taught exclusively at DePauw University from 1899 to 1910.

27. *Keramic Studio* 8 (March 1907): 240.

28. Postle, *Overbeck Pottery*, p. 26, mistakenly says she was twenty-three. Entries in the *American Art Annual* consistently give her birthdate as January 28, 1878.

29. Mary Overbeck, "Overbeck Pottery," p. 156.

30. Ibid.

31. They created some undecorated dinner sets as well as a number of small sculptured figurines. The latter were all hand-built, and some are delightfully humorous. Mary made a speciality of these in her later years, when she was alone. For this study and exhibition the bowls and vases only are featured. For exhibitions and awards, see Postle, *Overbeck Pottery*, p. 95.

32. Mayan art was known and adapted to designs of the 1920s and 1930s. See Marjorie I. Ingle, *The Mayan Revival Style: Art Deco Mayan Fantasy* (Salt Lake City: G. M. Smith, 1984).

33. Postle, *Overbeck Pottery*, p. 55. Her source is a now-lost typed manuscript by Elizabeth Overbeck, "The Chronicle of a Studio Pottery," ca. 1936.

34. Frederick Allen Whiting, "The Arts and Crafts at the Louisiana Purchase Exposition," *International Studio* 24 (November 1904): ccclxxxiv–cccxci.

35. "Louisiana Purchase Exposition Ceramics," *Keramic Studio* 6 (January 1905): 193–94; Ibid, (February 1905): 216–19; (March 1905): 251–52; (April 1905): 268–69; 7 (May 1905): 7–8.

36. *Official Catalogue of Exhibitors, Universal Exposition, Saint Louis, U.S.A. 1904, Division of Exhibits, Department of Art*, rev. ed. (Saint Louis: Official Catalogue Co., 1904), pp. 75–90. Le Boutillier (as collaborator with Grueby) and Binns received silver medals; Walrath received a bronze medal. See Florence N. Levy, ed., *American Art Annual, 1905–1906*, vol. 5 (New York: American Art Annual, 1905), p. 264. This source does not list all prizes; Joseph Meyer, potter at Newcomb, and other individuals received prizes in various divisions.

37. Elsie Binns, "Charles Fergus Binns, D. Sc.," *Alfred University Bulletin* 11 (November 1935): 7–22; Margaret Carney, *Charles Fergus Binns: The Father of American Studio Ceramics* (New York: Hudson Hills Press, Inc., 1998). Today's ceramists still use a "Binns Clear" glaze, some without knowing its source. Depending on the temperature of firing, it creates glazes from matte to glossy.

38. Adelaide Alsop Robineau probably studied with Binns in the spring of 1900, if not before. As early as 1901, she began experimenting in pottery modeling. By 1902–04 she was developing her own remarkable intricately carved porcelains, and continued to do so for the next two decades. Thus, she shaped her own career as an independent studio potter even as she continued to support and create designs for china painters. Martin Eidelberg, "Robineau's Early Designs," in Peg Weiss, ed., *Adelaide Alsop Robineau: Glory in Porcelain* (Syracuse, N.Y.: Syracuse University Press, 1981), pp. 43–92. Marshal Fry, who was to remain focused as a designer, attended summer school in 1901 at Alfred and gave an enthusiastic report. He subsequently served as an instructor for summer sessions. Marshal Fry, "Alfred Summer School of Ceramic Art," *Keramic Studio* 3 (December 1901): 165–66; Coy L. Ludwig, *The Arts and Crafts Movement in New York State, 1890s–1920s* (Hamilton, N.Y.: Gallery Association of New York State, 1984), p. 24.

39. New York: Scott, Greenwood & Son, 1901.

40. See Ludwig, *Arts and Crafts*, pp. 12–13, 15, 18; Clark, *Arts and Crafts*, pp. 180, 184; and Poesch, *Newcomb Pottery*, p. 95.

41. The Handicraft Shops were organized in 1904–05 by Dr. Herbert Hall, a pioneer in occupational therapy. He wanted to have "an industrial plant where he could send his nervously worn out patients for the blessing and privilege of quiet manual work."

42. See Herbert J. Hall, M. C., "Marblehead Pottery," *Keramic Studio* 10 (June 1908): 30–31; Arthur E. Baggs, "The Story of a Potter," *The Handicrafter* 1 (April/May 1910): 8–10; and Susan J. Montgomery, "The Potter's Art in Boston," in Marilee Boyd Meyer et al., *Inspired Reform: Boston's Arts and Crafts Movement* (Wellesley, Mass.: Davis Museum and Cultural Center in association with Bulfinch Press/Little, Brown and Company, 1997), pp. 62–64.

43. Poesch, *Newcomb Pottery*, pp. 73–86; 96–106.

44. Stephenson, "Newcomb College," p. 260.

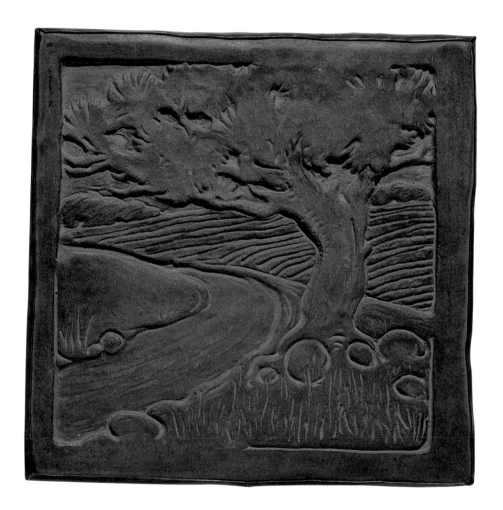

ERNEST BATCHELDER
Plaque, ca. 1910

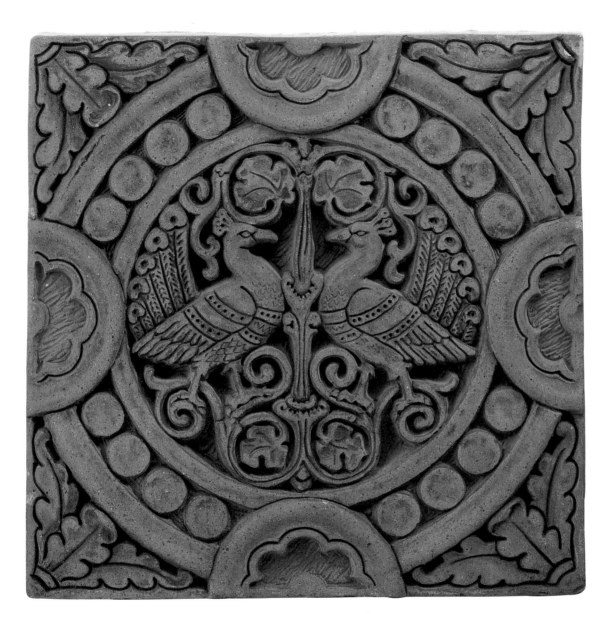

BATCHELDER-WILSON COMPANY
Tile (peacock in circle), ca. 1925

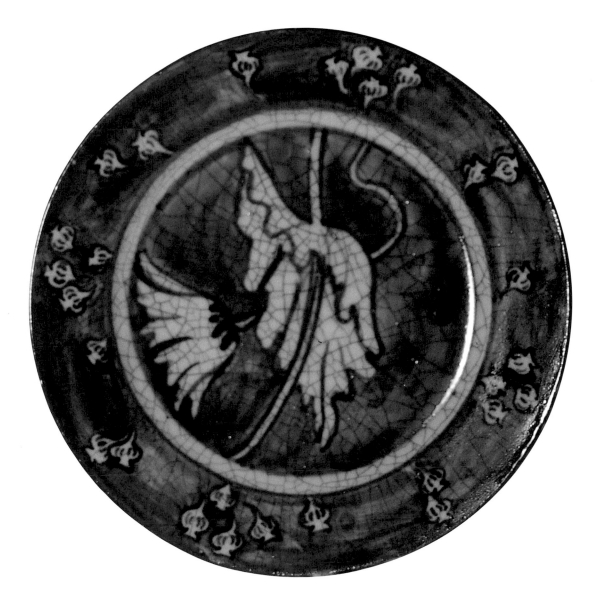

DEDHAM POTTERY
Plate (poppy design), 1895

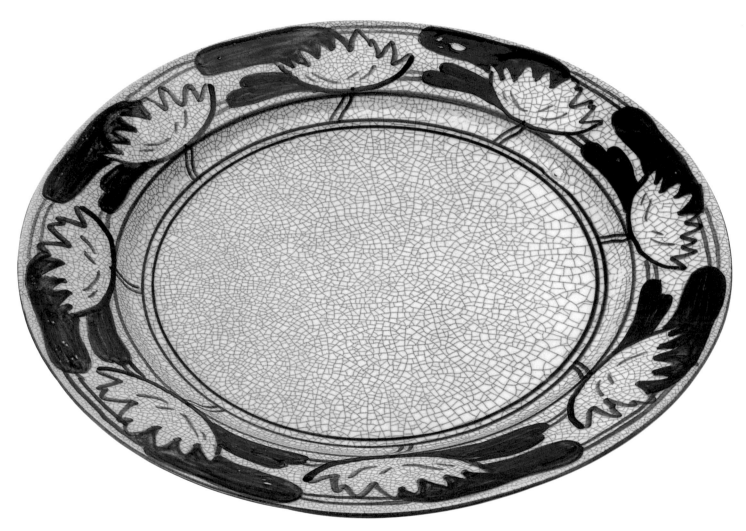

DEDHAM POTTERY
Plate (water-lily design), ca. 1910

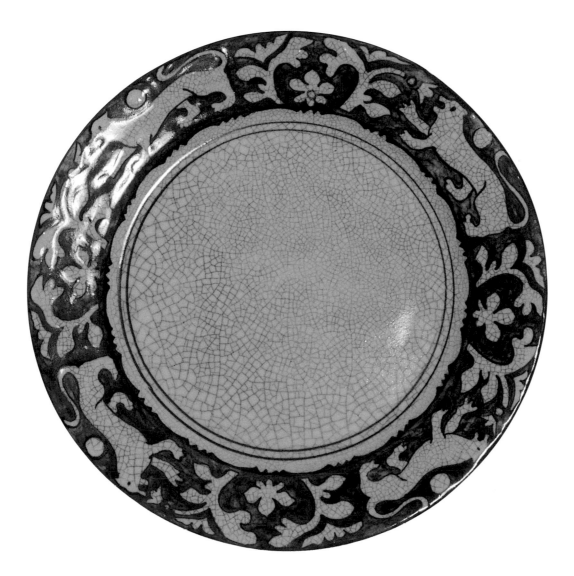

DEDHAM POTTERY
Plate (lion-pattern design), ca. 1920

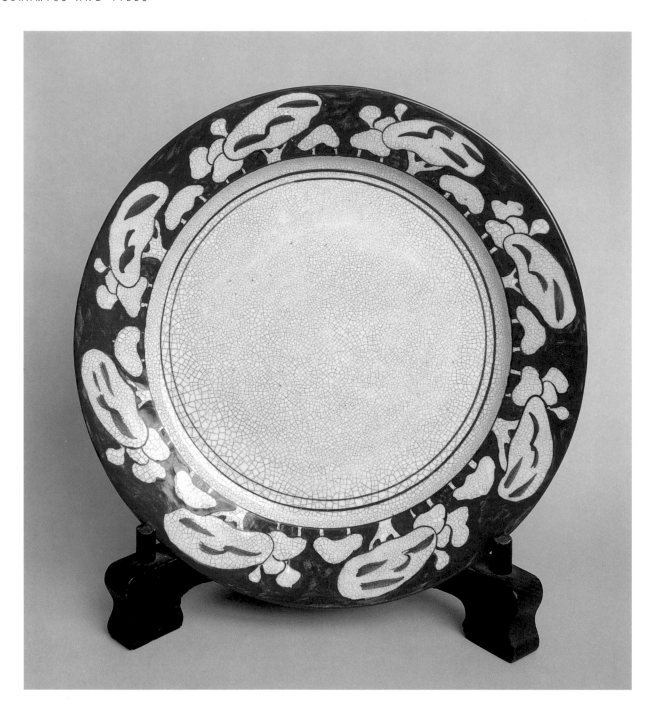

DEDHAM POTTERY
Plate (snow tree design), n.d.

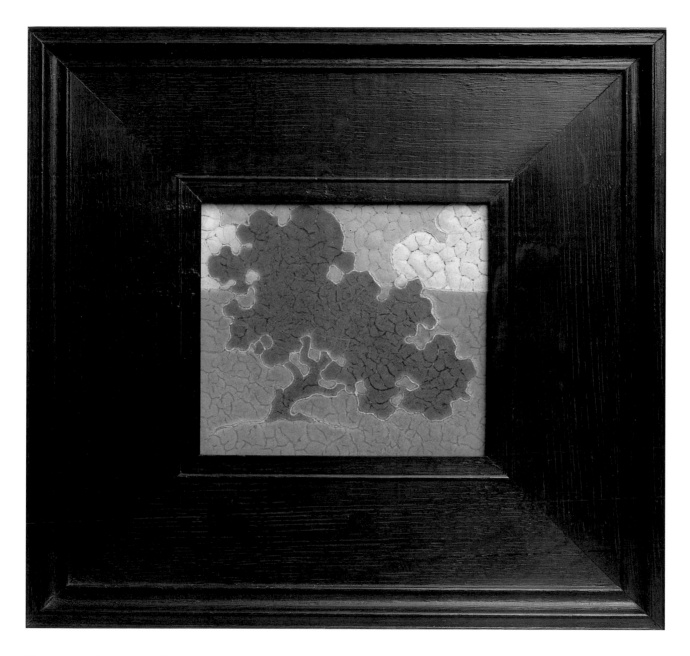

GRUEBY FAIENCE COMPANY
Tile (oak-tree design), ca. 1910

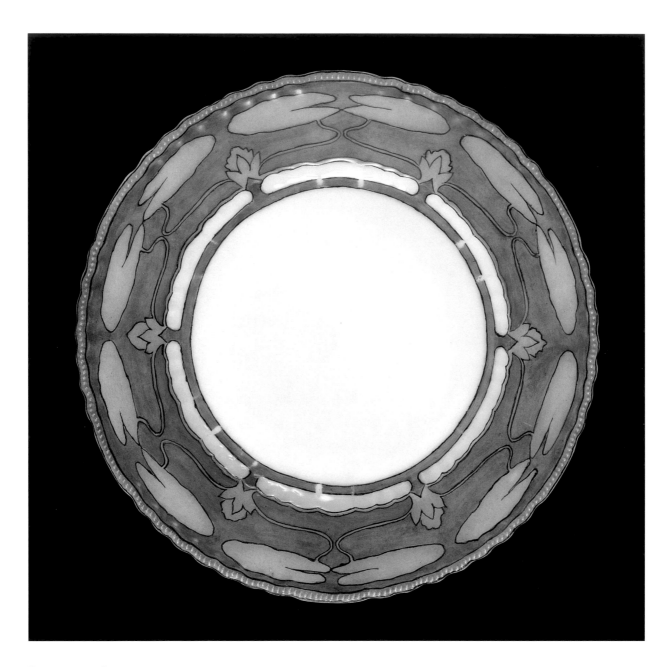

BLANCHE LAZZELL
Plate (flower and leaf design), 1907

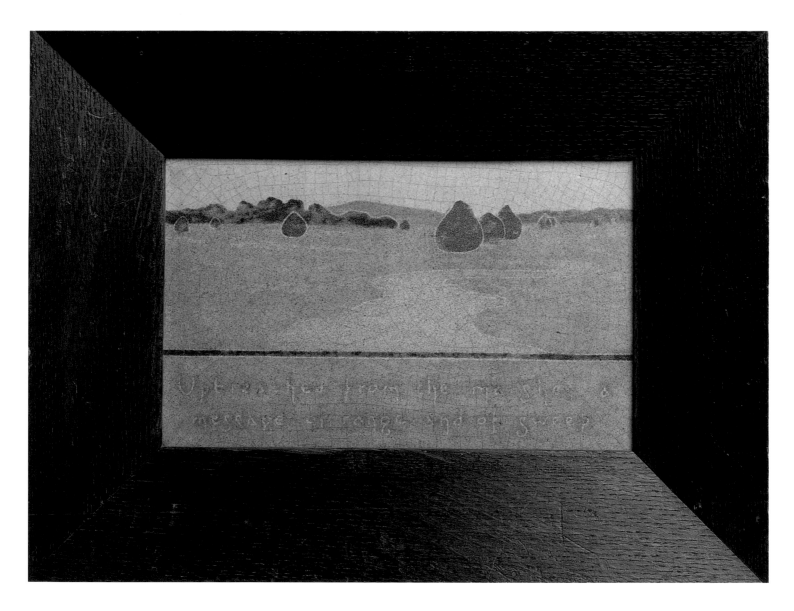

MARBLEHEAD POTTERY
Tile (marsh and tree design from a woodcut print
by Arthur W. Dow), ca. 1905

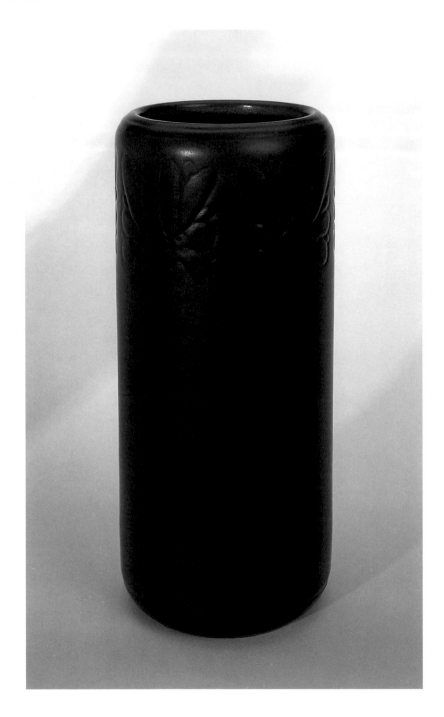

MARBLEHEAD POTTERY
Vase (tree design), ca. 1910

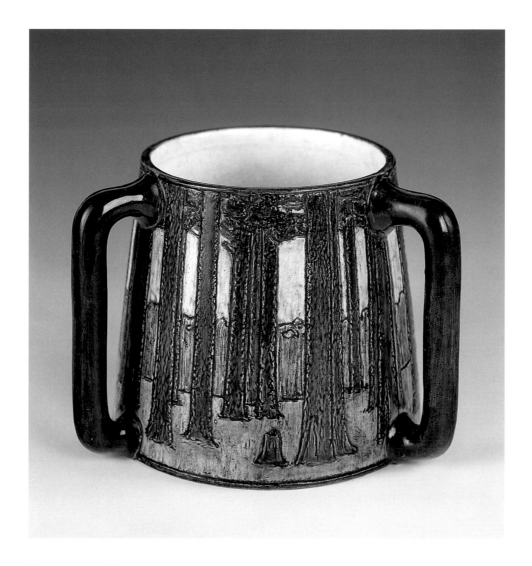

NEWCOMB POTTERY
Tyg (pine-grove design), ca. 1901

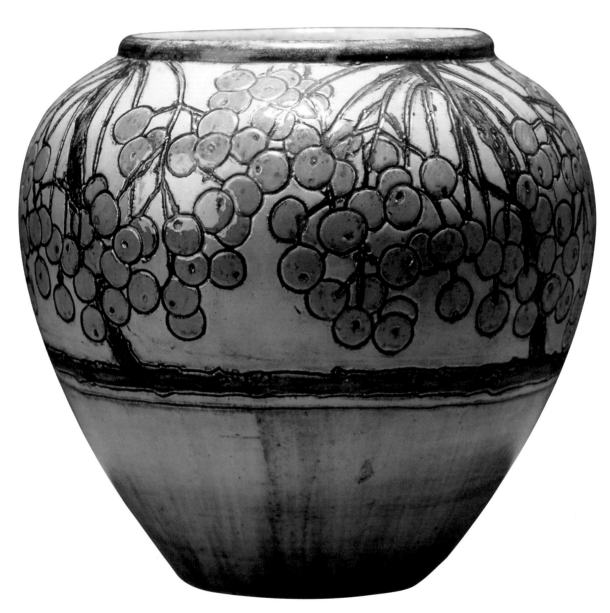

NEWCOMB POTTERY
Vase (chinaberry design), ca. 1902

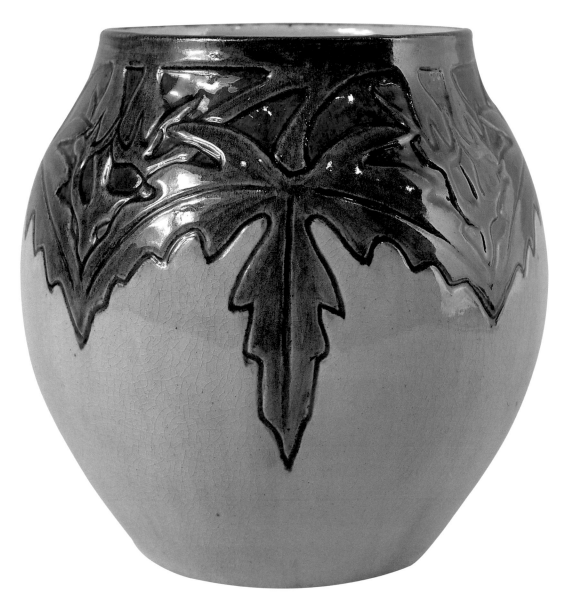

NEWCOMB POTTERY
Vase (leaf design), ca. 1903

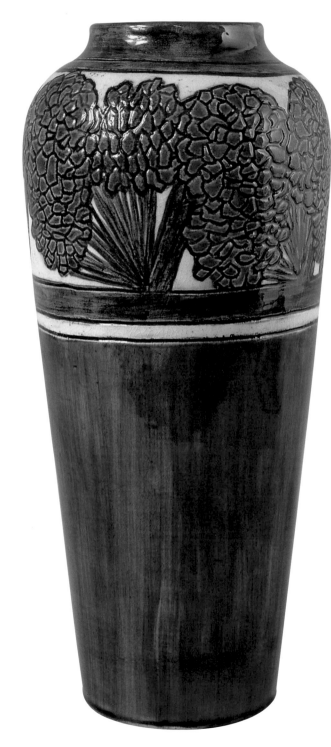

NEWCOMB POTTERY
Vase (hydrangea design), 1904

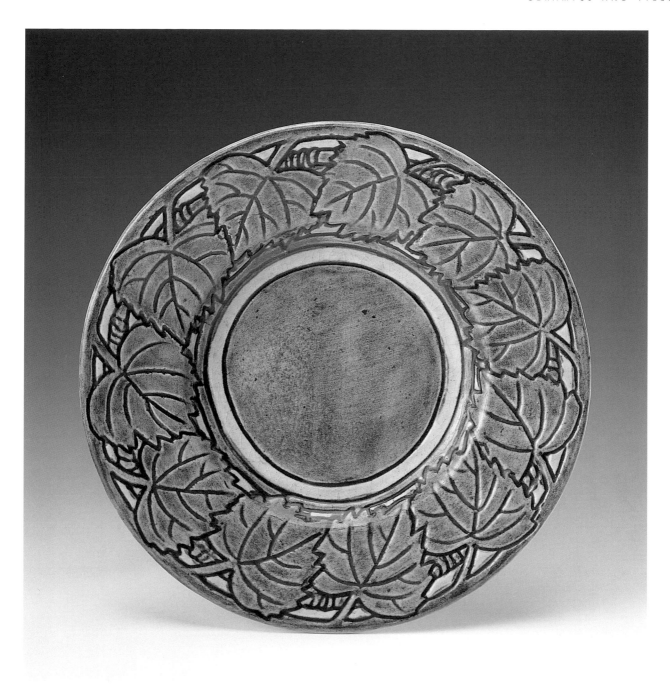

NEWCOMB POTTERY
Plate (leaf design), ca. 1904

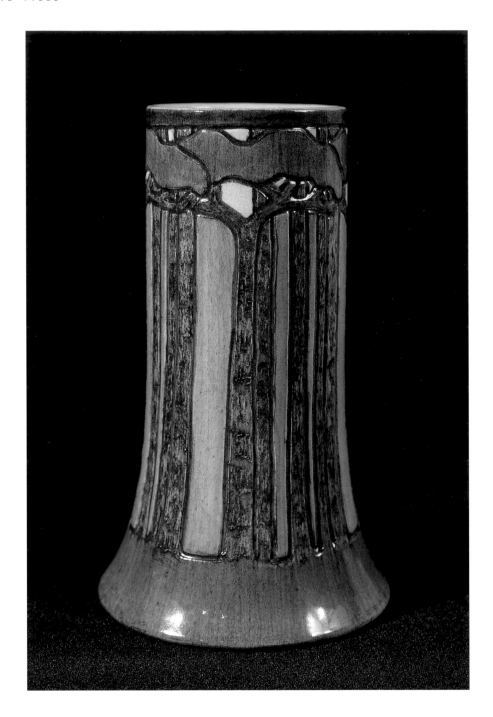

NEWCOMB POTTERY
Vase (pine-tree design), ca. 1905

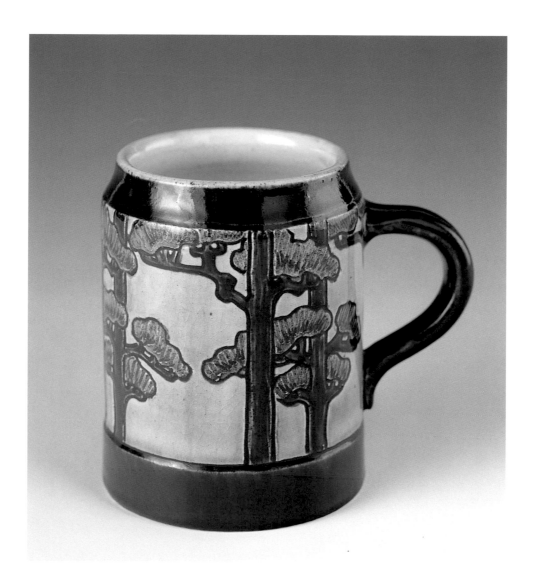

NEWCOMB POTTERY
Mug (southern-pine design), ca. 1905

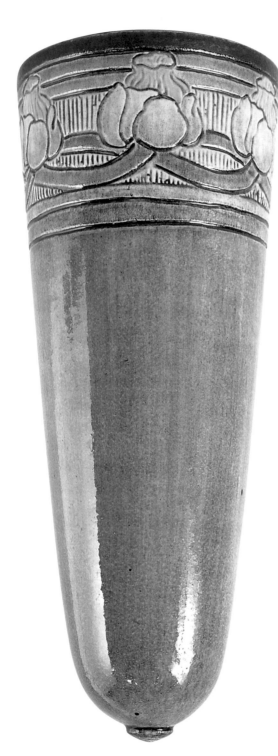

NEWCOMB POTTERY
Hanging Vase (lily design), ca. 1906

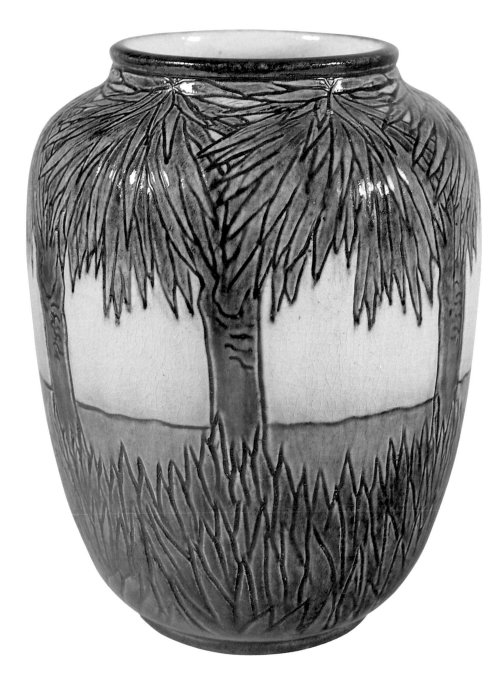

NEWCOMB POTTERY
Vase (yucca-tree design), ca. 1906

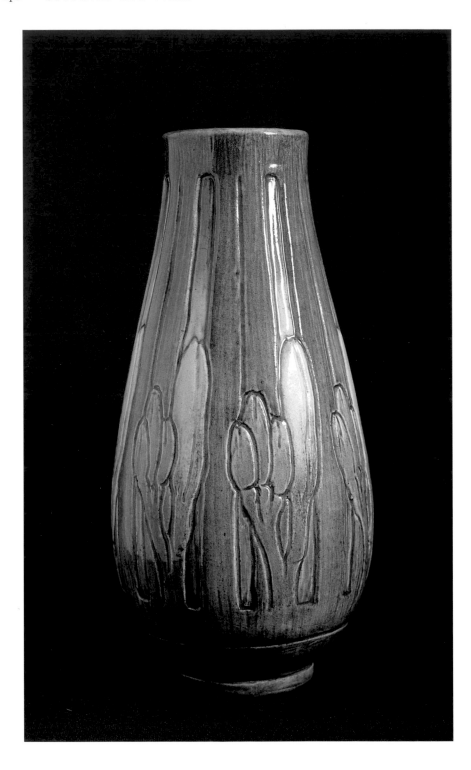

NEWCOMB POTTERY
Vase (lily design), ca. 1906

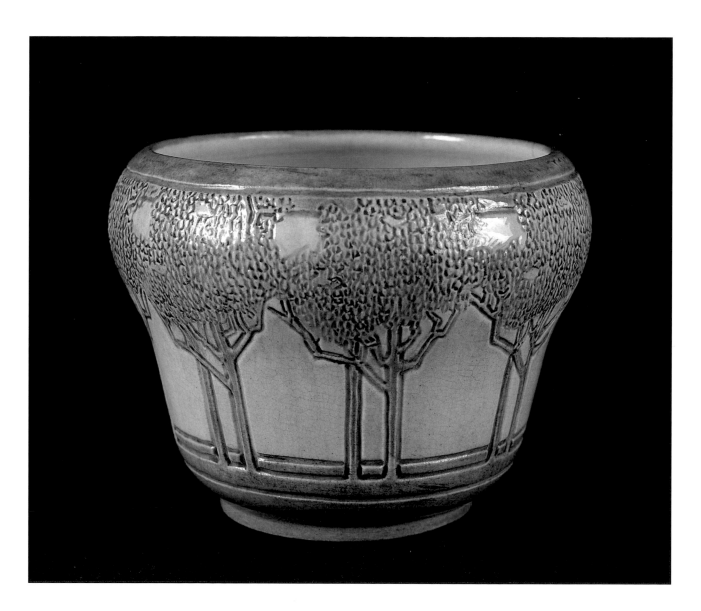

NEWCOMB POTTERY
Bowl (tree design), ca. 1907

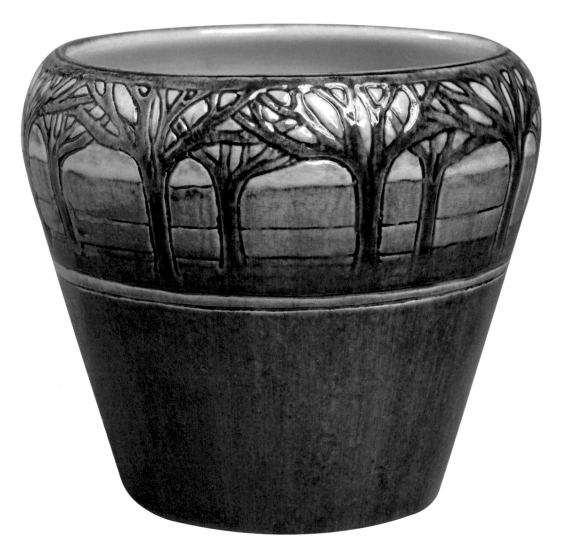

NEWCOMB POTTERY
Vase (china-ball tree design), ca. 1908

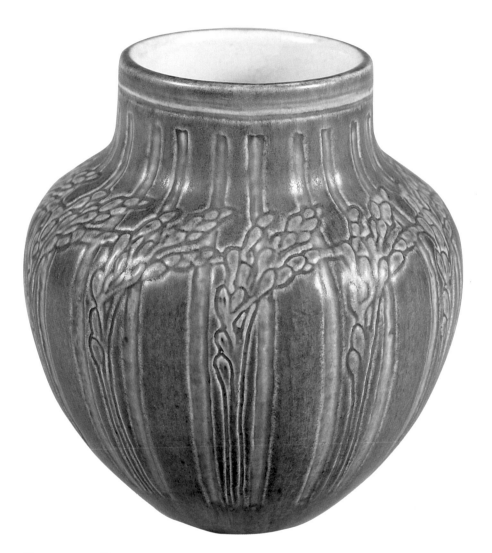

NEWCOMB POTTERY
Vase (rice design), ca. 1909

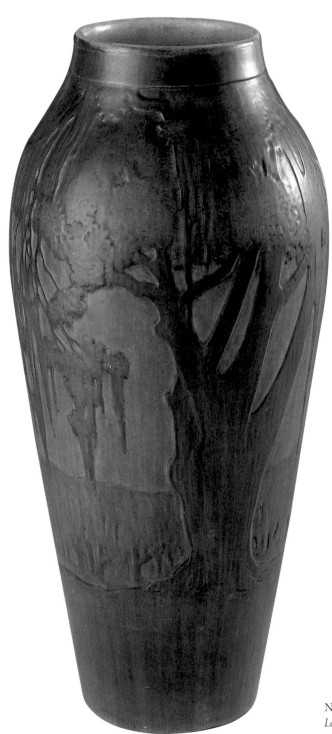

NEWCOMB POTTERY
Lamp Base (moon-drenched oak-tree design), ca. 1927

OVERBECK POTTERY
Vase (floral design), after 1911

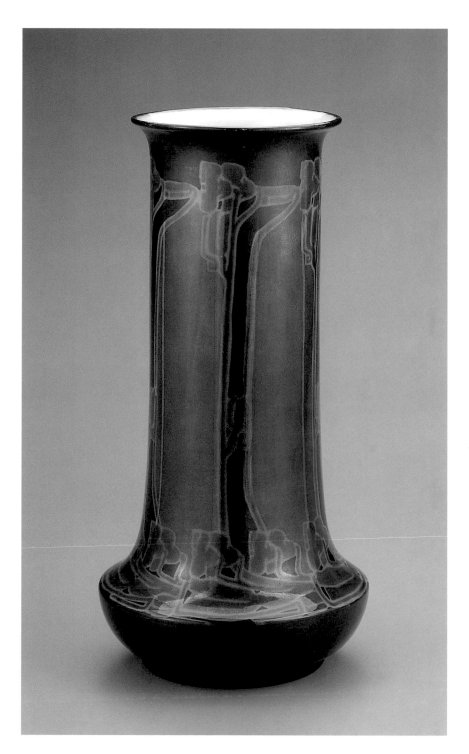

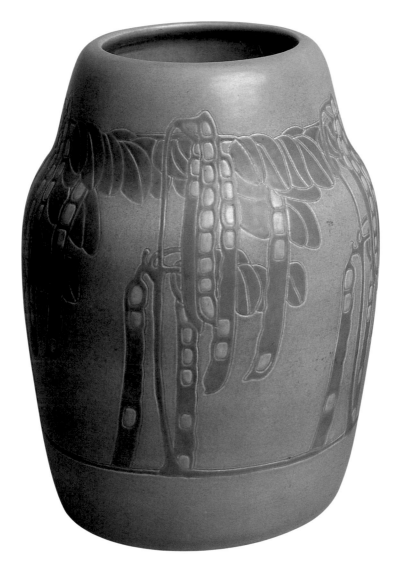

OVERBECK POTTERY
Vase (peapod design), after 1911

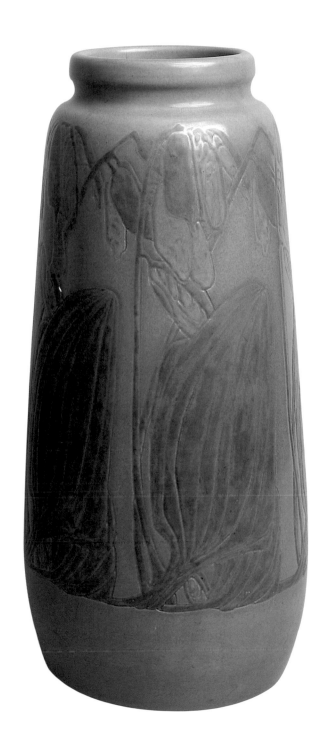

OVERBECK POTTERY
Vase (hosta design), after 1911

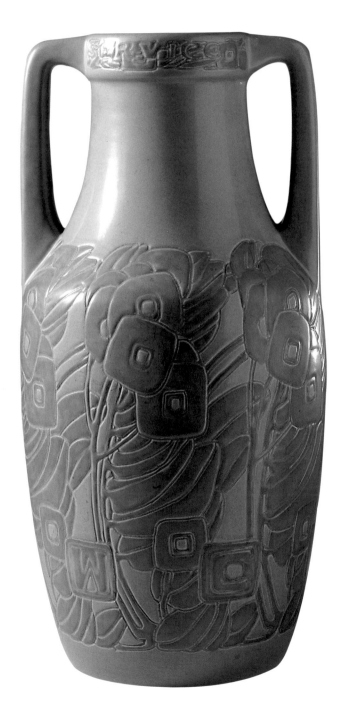

OVERBECK POTTERY
Trophy Cup (floral design), 1914

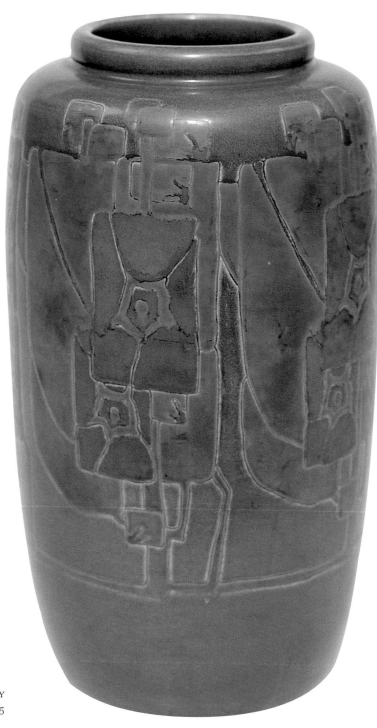

OVERBECK POTTERY
Vase (nasturtium design), 1915

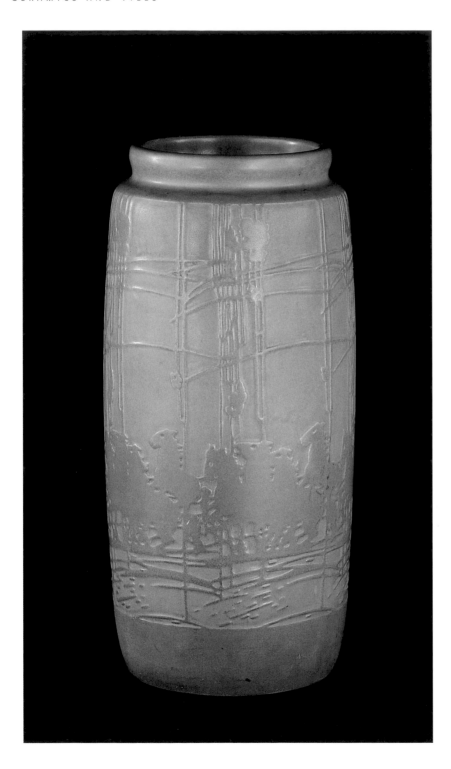

OVERBECK POTTERY
Vase, ca. 1915

OVERBECK POTTERY
Vase (gingko-leaf and deer design), n.d.

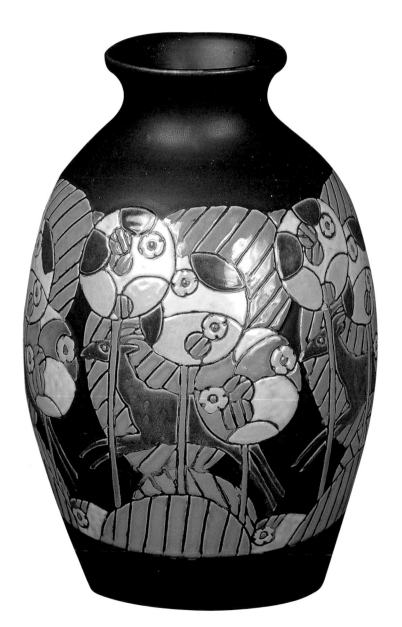

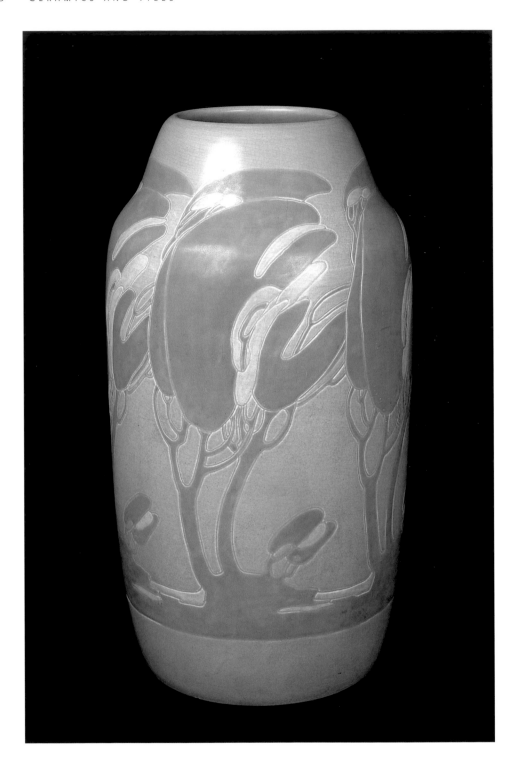

OVERBECK POTTERY
Vase (windblown-tree design), n.d.

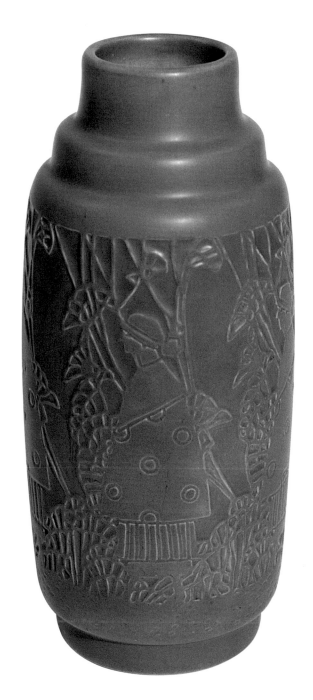

OVERBECK POTTERY
Vase (figurative design), n.d.

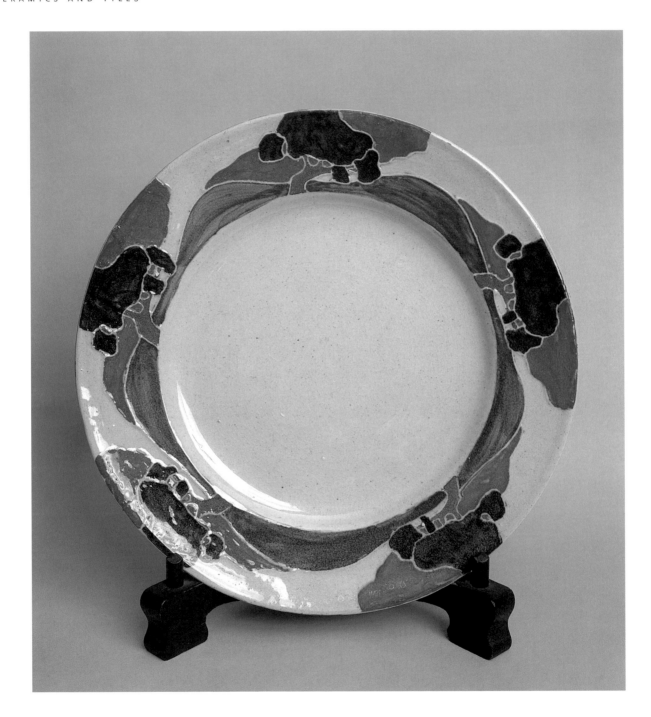

PEWABIC POTTERY
Plate, ca. 1905

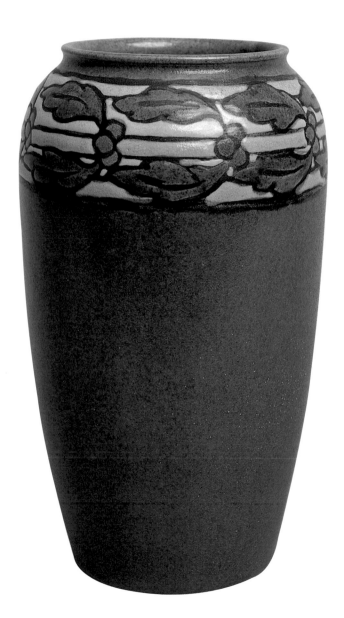

PAUL REVERE POTTERY OF THE
SATURDAY EVENING GIRLS' CLUB
Vase, ca. 1912

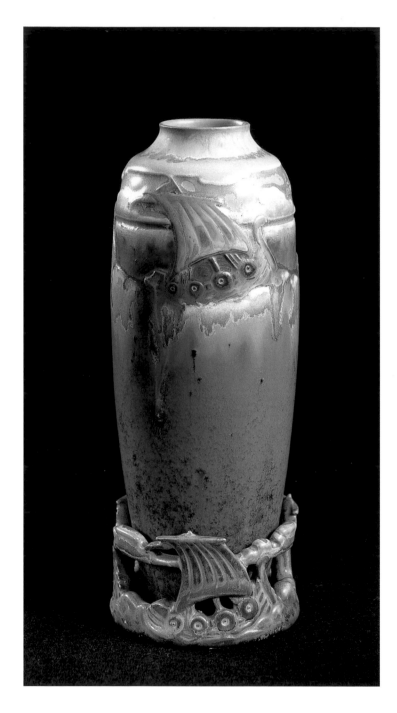

ADELAIDE ALSOP ROBINEAU
Vase (Viking-ship design), 1905

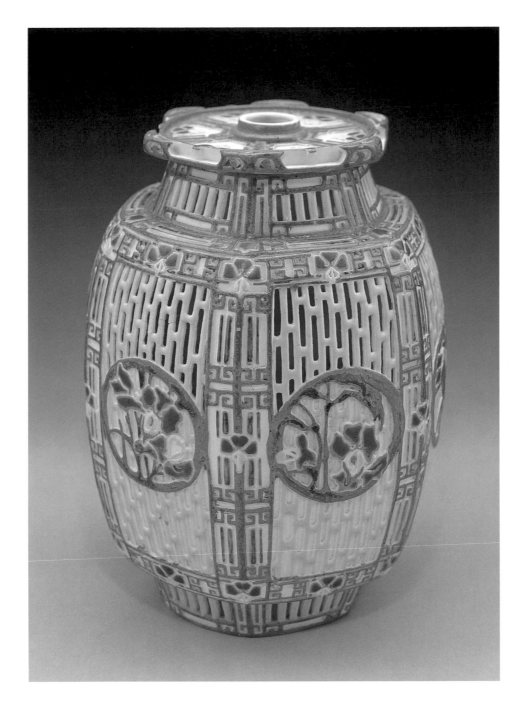

ADELAIDE ALSOP ROBINEAU
Lantern, 1908

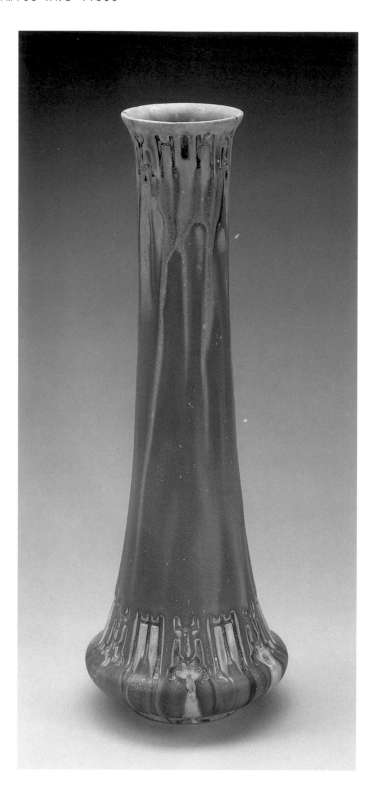

ADELAIDE ALSOP ROBINEAU
Vase (scarab design), before 1917

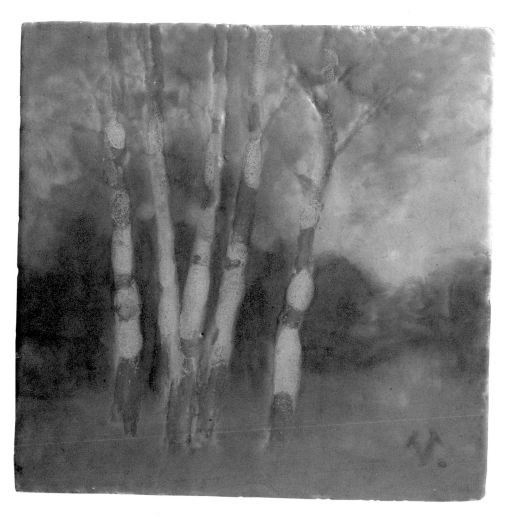

VOLKMAR KILNS
Tile (birch-tree design), ca. 1910

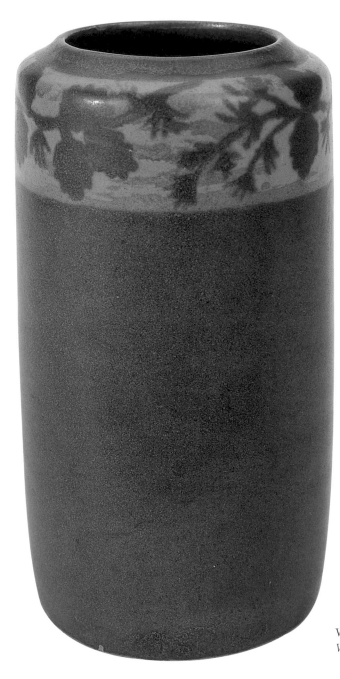

WALRATH POTTERY
Vase (pine-cone design), 1908–18

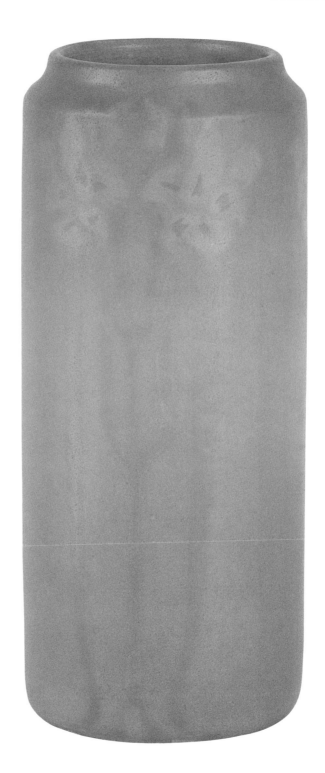

WALRATH POTTERY
Vase (floral design), ca. 1910

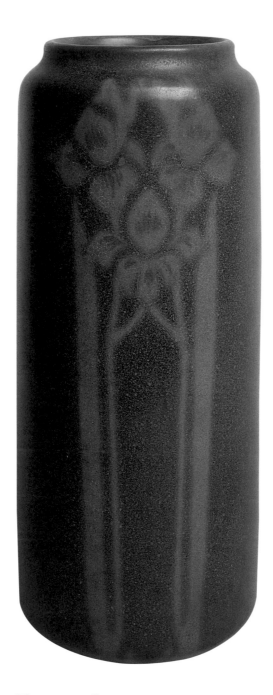

WALRATH POTTERY
Vase (iris design), ca. 1910

CHECKLIST OF THE EXHIBITION

MAUD AINSLIE (American, 1870–1960)

The Hat Shop, 1920
Color woodcut
H. 11 in.; W. 8½ in.
Provincetown Art Association & Museum (834.PR85)
(p. 10)

MARY FRANCES BAKER (American, 1879–1943)

Calendar, 1903
12 color woodcuts in hand-bound calendar
Each, H. 18 in.; W. 14 in.
Manuscript Department, Howard-Tilton Memorial
Library, Tulane University, New Orleans (522)
(p. 11)

ERNEST BATCHELDER (American, 1875–1957)

Plaque, ca. 1910
Terracotta
H. 8½ in.; W. 8½ in.; D. ¾ in.
Marks: incised *BATCHELDER*
Oakland Museum of California; Gift of Laetitia Meyer
(A68.63)
(p. 127)

BATCHELDER-WILSON COMPANY
(Pasadena, California, 1912–1932)

Tile (peacock in circle), ca. 1925
Press-molded fired clay with pigmented slip
H. 12¼ in.; W. 12¼ in.; D. 1 in.
Marks: impressed *3/Batchelder/Los A(ngele)s/3*
Oakland Museum of California; Gift of Terry W. Geiser
and Janet Mark (A94.5.1)
(p. 128)

JANET PAYNE BOWLES (American, 1882–1948)

Spoon, ca. 1912–15
Silver and pearl
H. 6½ in.; W. ½ in.; D. ¾ in.
Indianapolis Museum of Art; Gift of Jan and Mira
Bowles in memory of their mother, Janet Payne Bowles
(68.21.99)
(p. 182)

Ladle, ca. 1916–19
Silver and gold wash
H. 11¾ in.; W. 3⅜ in.; Dia. 2½ in.
Indianapolis Museum of Art; Gift of Jan and Mira
Bowles in memory of their mother, Janet Payne Bowles
(68.21.11)
(p. 182)

BYRDCLIFFE COLONY
(Woodstock, New York, opened 1903)

Linen Press, ca. 1904
Oak with metal hinges
H. 72¾ in.; W. 54 in.; D. 24 in.
Cathers & Dembrosky, New York
(p. 183)

Chest, ca. 1904
Oak with metal hinges
H. 20 in.; W. 50 in.; D. 22 in.
Cathers & Dembrosky, New York
(p. 184)

Chest, ca. 1904
Oak with polychrome panels
H. 60 in.; W. 57 in.; D. 23¾ in.
Collection Mark and Jill Willcox, courtesy
Robert Edwards
(p. 185)

Cabinet, ca. 1904
Panels by Herman Dudley Murphy
Oak with polychrome panels
H. 27¼ in.; W. 38 in.; D. 14¾ in.
Collection Mark and Jill Willcox, courtesy
Robert Edwards
(p. 186)

Hanging Cabinet, n.d.
Panels by Zulma Steele
Oak with carved and polychrome panels
H. 14 in.; W. 42½ in.; D. 8 in.
Collection Mark and Jill Willcox, courtesy of
Robert Edwards
(p. 187)

ALVIN LANGDON COBURN
(American, 1882–1966)

The Pier, 1903
Gum bichromate over platinum print
H. 6½ in.; W. 4⅛ in.
The Metropolitan Museum of Art; The Alfred Stieglitz
Collection 1933 (33.43.192)
(p. 87)

The Bridges-Ipswich, 1904
Photogravure
H. 7⅝ in.; W. 5⅞ in.
Minneapolis Institute of the Arts; Gift of Julia Marshall
(69-133.6.5)
(p. 87)

Grand Canyon, 1912
Platinum print
H. 11 in.; W. 14 in.
Private collection, courtesy Janet Lehr, Inc., New York
(p. 88)

Grand Canyon, 1912
Platinum print
H. 14 in.; W. 11 in.
Private collection, courtesy Janet Lehr, Inc., New York
(p. 89)

Untitled (water and windblown tree), ca. 1915
From the Welsh series
Watercolor
H. 5¾ in.; W. 8⁹⁄₁₆ in.
Private collection, courtesy Janet Lehr, Inc., New York
(p. 12)

Untitled (landscape with mountain and dune), ca. 1915
From the Welsh series
Watercolor
H. 5¾ in.; W. 8⁹⁄₁₆ in.
Private collection, courtesy Janet Lehr, Inc., New York
(p. 13)

DEDHAM POTTERY
(Dedham, Massachusetts, 1895–1943)

Plate (poppy design), 1895
Stoneware
Dia. 8½ in.
Marks: impressed rabbit design
Collection James D. Kaufman
(p. 129)

Plate (water-lily design), ca. 1910
Stoneware
Dia. 10 in.
Marks: square, blue stamped rabbit design
Collection Alexandra Sheldon
(p. 130)

Plate (lion-pattern design), ca. 1920
Designed by Denman Ross
Decorated by Maude R. Davenport
Stoneware
Dia. 8⁷⁄₁₆ in.
Marks: square, blue stamped rabbit design
Collection James D. Kaufman
(p. 131)

Plate (snow tree design), n.d.
Stoneware
Dia. 10 in.
Marks: impressed rabbit design
Collection Stephen Gray
(p. 132)

ARTHUR WESLEY DOW (American, 1857–1922)

Modern Art, 1895
Color lithograph
H. 17¾ in.; W. 13¹¹/₁₆ in.
Collection Andrew Terry Keats
(p. 14)

A Bend in the River, ca. 1895
Color woodcut
H. 5 in; W. 2¼ in.
Collection George and Barbara Wright
(p. 15)

Bend in a River, ca. 1895
Color woodcut
H. 7³/₁₆ in.; W. 2⅞ in.
Herbert F. Johnson Museum of Art, Cornell University;
Gift of Robert and Esther Doherty (98.051.002)
(p. 15)

Silhouetted Trees, ca. 1895–1910
Cyanotype
H. 6⅜ in.; W. 8⅜ in.
Museum of Fine Arts, Boston; Jesse H. Wilkinson Fund
(1997.107)
(p. 90)

Japanese Color Prints, 1896
Color lithograph
H. 23½ in.; W. 17¾ in.
The Rare Book and Manuscript Library of Columbia
University; Solton and Julia Engel Collection
(p. 16)

The Lotos, 1896
Color lithograph
H. 11¹³/₁₆ in.; W. 9¹³/₁₆ in.
The Rare Book and Manuscript Library of Columbia
University; Solton and Julia Engel Collection
(p. 16)

August Moon, ca. 1905
Color woodcut
H. 4½ in.; W. 7⅛ in.
Collection Theodore B. Donson and Marvel M. Griepp
(p. 17)

Marsh Creek, ca. 1905
Color woodcut
H. 4¼ in.; W. 7 in.
Herbert F. Johnson Museum of Art, Cornell University;
Marcel K. Sessler (Class of 1913) Fund (89.001)
(p. 17)

Rain in May, ca. 1907
Color woodcut
H. 6⅛ in.; W. 5 in.
Collection Stephen Gray
(p. 18)

Bend of a River (Sunset), ca. 1908
Color woodcut
H. 4½ in.; W. 7 in.
Museum of Fine Arts, Boston; Gift of Mrs. Ethelwyn H.
Putnam (41.715)
(p. 19)

On Yavapai Trail, 1911
Silver print
H. 14 in.; W. 11 in.
Collection George and Barbara Wright
(p. 91)

Pacific Grove, 1912
Silver print
H. 11 in.; W. 14 in.
Collection George and Barbara Wright
(p. 92)

Composition: A Series of Exercises in Art Structure for the Use of Students and Teachers
New York: Doubleday, Page and Co., 1913 (first
edition 1899)
H. 11⅝ in.; W. 9½ in.; D. ⅝ in.
Private collection
(p. 188)

The Derelict (The Lost Boat), 1916
Color woodcut
H. 5¹³/₁₆ in.; W. 4⅝ in.
Amon Carter Museum, Fort Worth, Texas (1988.30)
(p. 20)

Willows in Bloom, n.d.
Color woodcut
H. 4½ in.; W. 2½ in.
Collection George and Barbara Wright
(p. 20)

The Dragon, n.d.
Cyanotype
H. 6 in.; W. 8 in.
Collection George and Barbara Wright
(p. 93)

FRANK MORLEY FLETCHER (British, 1866–1949)

The Bookworm, ca. 1920–25
Color woodcut
H. 7⁹⁄₁₆ in.; W. 6³⁄₁₆ in.
San Diego Museum of Art; Gift of the University
Women's Club (1931:050)
(p. 21)

California. 2. Mount Shasta, ca. 1930
Color woodcut
H. 9⅝ in.; W. 13½ in.
Fine Arts Museums of San Francisco, Achenbach
Foundation for Graphic Arts; Gift of Mr. and
Mrs. F. A. Lejeune (1976.1.354)
(p. 22)

California. 3. Ojai Valley, ca. 1935
Color woodcut
H. 11½ in.; W. 9 in.
Collection Stephen Gray
(p. 23)

ELIZA DRAPER GARDINER (American, 1871–1955)

Pick-A-Back, ca. 1919
Color woodcut
H. 8 in.; W. 10 in.
Collection Peter Falk
(p. 24)

Passconaway, ca. 1919
Color woodcut
H. 7¼ in.; W. 10 in.
Collection Peter Falk
(p. 25)

FRANCES H. GEARHART (American, 1869–1956)

Old Pine, ca. 1922
Color woodcut
H. 11½ in.; W. 10 in.
Herbert F. Johnson Museum of Art, Cornell University;
Purchased with funds generously donated by Phyllis
Goody Cohen, Class of 1957 (93.023)
(p. 26)

High Blues, n.d.
Color woodcut
H. 9⅞ in.; W. 8⅞ in.
Collection Stephen Gray
(p. 27)

GRUEBY FAIENCE COMPANY
(Boston, 1894–1919)

Tile (oak-tree design), ca. 1910
Earthenware
H. 8 in.; W. 8 in.
Marks: none
Private collection
(p. 133)

EDNA BEL BOIES HOPKINS
(American, 1872–1937)

Eucalyptus, ca. 1910
Color woodcut
H. 10⅞ in.; W. 7⅛ in.
Print Collection, Miriam and Ira D. Wallach Division
of Art, Prints, and Photographs, The New York Public
Library; Astor, Lenox, and Tilden Foundations
(p. 28)

Morning Glory, ca. 1915
Color woodcut
H. 11 in.; W. 7⅛ in.
Herbert F. Johnson Museum of Art, Cornell University;
Bequest of William P. Chapman, Jr., Class of 1895
(62.2350)
(p. 28)

JAMES HOPKINS (American, 1877–1969)

Untitled (mountain scene), ca. 1915
Color woodcut
H. 8¾ in.; W. 10⅝ in.
Herbert F. Johnson Museum of Art, Cornell University;
Membership Purchase Fund (90.015)
(p. 29)

HELEN HYDE (American, 1868–1919)

Mount Orizaba, 1912
Color woodcut
H. 9½ in.; W. 9 in.
Herbert F. Johnson Museum of Art, Cornell University;
Bequest of William P. Chapman, Jr., Class of 1895
(62.2362)
(p. 30)

SADIE IRVINE (American, 1887–1970)

Garden Party, ca. 1930
Color woodcut
H. 12⅝ in.; W. 9¾ in.
Louisiana State Museum (1979.72.462)
(p. 31)

Marsh Maple, ca. 1930
Color woodcut
H. 11¼ in.; W. 7⅛ in.
Louisiana State Museum (1979.72.18)
(p. 31)

JANE BERRY JUDSON (American, 1869–1935)

A Bit of the Forest of Fontainebleau, 1910s
Color woodcut
H. 5¾ in.; W. 8 in.
Private collection
(p. 32)

Twilight: Sheepscot River, Maine, 1910s
Color woodcut
H. 7⅞ in.; W. 5⅞ in.
Herbert F. Johnson Museum of Art, Cornell University;
Gift of Richard Barons (97.030)
(p. 33)

GERTRUDE KÄSEBIER (American, 1852–1934)

The Road to Rome, 1903
Gum bichromate print
H. 9¼ in.; W. 13⅛ in.
George Eastman House, Rochester, New York
(70:0058:0016)
(p. 94)

Fishing Banks: Newfoundland, 1912
Platinum print
H. 7⅝ in.; W. 9½ in.
George Eastman House, Rochester, New York
(74:060:30)
(p. 95)

JOSEPH T. KEILEY (American, 1869–1914)

Landscape, ca. 1900
Platinum print
H. 4⅝ in.; W. 2¼ in.
The Art Museum, Princeton University; Gift of the Estate
of John Emlen Bullock (1973–90)
Copyright 1998 Photo: Trustees of Princeton University
(p. 96)

Reverie: The Last Hour, 1901
Platinum print
H. 4⅜ in.; W. 7⅜ in.
The Metropolitan Museum of Art; The Alfred Stieglitz
Collection, 1933 (33.43.170)
(p. 97)

From a New York Ferryboat, 1904
Platinum print
H. 3⅝ in.; W. 4½ in.
The Metropolitan Museum of Art; The Alfred Stieglitz
Collection, 1933 (33.43.178)
(p. 97)

BLANCHE LAZZELL (American, 1878–1956)

Plate (flower and leaf design), 1907
Hand-painted porcelain
Dia. 8 in.
Marks: *Blanche Lazzell, 1907*
Collection Leslie and Joanna Garfield
(p. 134)

PEDRO DE LEMOS (American, 1882–1945)

Old Pines at Monterey, ca. 1915
Color woodcut
H. 5⅜ in.; W. 11⅝ in.
Collection Andrew Terry Keats
(p. 34)

Hillside Harvest, ca. 1920
Color woodcut
H. 8 in.; W. 6½ in.
Collection Andrew Terry Keats
(p. 35)

The Art Teacher: A Book for Children and Teachers
Worcester, Massachusetts: The Davis Press, 1949
H. 9 in.; W. 6½ in.; D. 1¼ in.
Private collection
(p. 189)

BERTHA LUM (American, 1879–1954)

Rain, 1913
Color woodcut
H. 11 in.; W. 6¼ in.
Private collection
(p. 36)

MARBLEHEAD POTTERY
(Marblehead, Massachusetts, 1904–1936)

Tile (marsh and tree design from a woodcut print
by Arthur W. Dow), ca. 1905
Designed by Arthur E. Baggs
Earthenware
H: 14 in.; W. 10½ in.
Marks: *AB*
Private collection
(p. 135)

Vase (tree design), ca. 1910
Earthenware
H. 8⅞ in.; Dia. 5 in.
Marks: Marblehead ship design
Collection Alexandra Sheldon
(p. 136)

NEWCOMB POTTERY (New Orleans, 1895–1940)

Tyg (pine-grove design), ca. 1901
Thrown by Joseph Meyer
Decorated by Harriet Joor
Earthenware
H. 5⅞ in.; W. 6⁹⁄₁₆ in.
Marks: *N* within *C* cipher; conjoined cipher of *JM*;
conjoined cipher of *HJ*; *U*; *S 28*
H. Sophie Newcomb College, Tulane University;
Gift of Mrs. Marshall B. Stewart (C.1996.38.A)
(p. 137)

Vase (chinaberry design), ca. 1902
Thrown by Joseph Meyer
Decorated by Harriet Joor
Earthenware
H. 7⅞ in.; W. 8½ in.
Marks: *N* within *C* cipher; conjoined cipher of *JM*; *Q*;
painted, conjoined cipher of *HJ* and *R 33*; incised,
conjoined cipher of *HJ*
New Orleans Museum of Art; Gift of Newcomb College
(38.29)
(p. 138)

Vase (leaf design), ca. 1903
Thrown by Joseph Meyer
Decorated by Roberta Kennon
Earthenware
H. 8 in.; Dia. 7¾ in.
Marks: *N* within *C* cipher; conjoined cipher of *JM*;
within rectangle, *R.B.K.*; *Z 77*
On loan to the Louisiana State Museum; courtesy
Newcomb Art Department, H. Sophie Newcomb College
of Tulane University (6087)
(p. 139)

Vase (hydrangea design), 1904
Thrown by Joseph Meyer
Decorated by Harriet Joor
Earthenware
H. 11½ in.; W. 2½ in.; Dia. 4⅛ in
Marks: on bottom, *N* within *C* cipher; conjoined cipher
of *HJ*; conjoined cipher of *JM*; *TT 55*; *W*
Louisiana State Museum (1975.1.4)
(p. 140)

Plate (leaf design), ca. 1904
Thrown by Joseph Meyer
Decorated by Harriet Joor
Earthenware
H. 1 in.; Dia. 9¹/₁₆ in.
Marks: *N* within *C* cipher; conjoined cipher of *JM*;
conjoined cipher of *HJ*; *Q*; *YY 78*
H. Sophie Newcomb College, Tulane University
(1973.61.A)
(p. 141)

Vase (pine-tree design), ca. 1905
Thrown by Joseph Meyer
Decorated by Roberta Kennon
Earthenware
H. 9 in.; Dia. 5½ in.
Marks. *N* within *C* cipher; conjoined cipher of *JM*; *Q*;
RBK; *AQ 45*
On loan to the Louisiana State Museum; courtesy
Newcomb Art Department, H. Sophie Newcomb
College, Tulane University (6116)
(p. 142)

Mug (southern-pine design), ca. 1905
Thrown by Joseph Meyer
Decorated by Desiree Roman
Earthenware
H. 4¼ in.; Dia. 4½ in. at handle
Marks: *N* within *C* cipher; conjoined cipher of *JM*; *Q*;
incised and painted cipher of *D.R.*; painted *AK 95*
H. Sophie Newcomb College, Tulane University (6117)
(p. 143)

Hanging Vase (lily design), ca. 1906
Thrown by Joseph Meyer
Decorated by Amelie Roman
Earthenware
H. 10 in.; Dia. 3½ in.
Marks: inside vase, *N* within *C* cipher; conjoined cipher
of *JM*; *AR*; *Q*; *BI* [or *BT*] 26
Louisiana State Museum (1975.1.20)
(p. 144)

Vase (yucca-tree design), ca. 1906
Thrown by Joseph Meyer
Decorated by Marie de Hoa LeBlanc
Earthenware
H. 8¼ in.; Dia. 6½ in.
Marks: *N* within *C* cipher; conjoined cipher of *JM*; *MHLeB*;
BE 49
New Orleans Museum of Art; Gift of Newcomb College
(38.18)
(p. 145)

Vase (lily design), ca. 1906
Thrown by Joseph Meyer
Decorated by Marie de Hoa LeBlanc
Earthenware
H. 8¼ in.; Dia. 4 in.
Marks: *N* within *C* cipher; *Q*; conjoined cipher of
MHLeD; *BJ 43*
On loan to the Louisiana State Museum, courtesy
Newcomb Art Department, H. Sophie Newcomb
College, Tulane University (6091)
(p. 146)

Bowl (tree design), ca. 1907
Thrown by Joseph Meyer
Decorated by Marie Levering Benson
Earthenware
H. 5¾ in.; Dia. 7¼ in.
Marks: *N* within *C* cipher; conjoined cipher of *JM*;
conjoined cipher of *MLB*; *BT 39*; *Q*
On loan to the Louisiana State Museum, courtesy of
the Newcomb Art Department, H. Sophie Newcomb
College, Tulane University (6102)
(p. 147)

Vase (china-ball tree design), ca. 1908
Thrown by Joseph Meyer
Decorated by Marie de Hoa LeBlanc
Earthenware
H. 5½ in.; Dia. 6½ in.
Marks: impressed cipher of *NC* stained blue; incised
cipher of *MHLeB* stained blue; impressed cipher
of *JM*; *CJ*
The Newark Museum; Purchase 1911 (11.498)
(p. 148)

Vase (rice design), ca. 1909
Thrown by Joseph Meyer
Decorated by Henrietta Bailey
Earthenware
H. 5¾ in.; Dia. 5½ in.
Marks: *N* within *C* cipher; conjoined cipher of *JM*;
conjoined cipher of *HB*; *DG 28*
New Orleans Museum of Art; Gift of H. Sophie
Newcomb College (38.12)
(p. 149)

Lamp Base (moon-drenched oak-tree design), ca. 1927
Thrown by Joseph Meyer
Decorated by Sadie Irvine
Earthenware
H. 16¹¹⁄₁₆ in.; Dia. 7⁷⁄₁₆ at shoulder
Marks: *N* within *C* cipher; conjoined cipher of *JM*;
scripted *S*; *142*; *QH 69*
H. Sophie Newcomb College, Tulane University
(C.1973.124.A)
(p. 150)

BROR NORDFELDT
(American, born in Sweden, 1878–1955)

The Skyrocket, 1906
Color woodcut
H. 8¾ in.; W. 11¼ in.
Amon Carter Museum, Fort Worth, Texas (1985.300)
(p. 37)

Pussy Willows, 1906
Color woodcut
H. 7½ in.; W. 9½ in.
Print Collection, Miriam and Ira D. Wallach Division of
Art, Prints, and Photographs, The New York Public
Library, Astor, Lenox, and Tilden Foundations
(p. 37)

GEORGIA O'KEEFFE (American, 1887–1986)

Lady with Red Hair, ca. 1914–16
Color linocut
H. 7½ in.; W. 7 in.
Gerald Peters Gallery, Santa Fe
Copyright Private Collection and The Georgia O'Keeffe
Foundation
(p. 38)

Red and Blue Mountains, ca. 1917
Watercolor
H. 11¼ in.; W. 7½ in.
Gerald Peters Gallery, Santa Fe
Copyright Private Collection and The Georgia O'Keeffe
Foundation
(p. 39)

OVERBECK POTTERY
(Cambridge City, Indiana, 1911–1955)

Vase (floral design), after 1911
Thrown by Elizabeth Gray Overbeck
Decorated by Hannah Borger Overbeck
Porcelain and polychrome enamel
H. 11⅝ in.; Dia. 5⅛ in.
Marks: on bottom in blue, *Hannah B. Overbeck*
Indianapolis Museum of Art; Institute of Business
Designers, Indiana Chapter Fund (1993.87)
(p. 151)

Vase (peapod design), after 1911
Thrown by Elizabeth Gray Overbeck
Decorated by Mary Frances Overbeck
Earthenware
H. 10 in.; Dia. 7 in.
Marks: stylized ciphers of *OBK* and *EF*
Collection Stephen Gray
(p. 152)

Vase (hosta design), after 1911
Thrown by Elizabeth Gray Overbeck
Decorated by Mary Frances Overbeck
Earthenware
H. 14¼ in.; Dia. 7 in.
Marks: stylized ciphers of *OBK* and *EF*
Collection Stephen Gray
(p. 153)

Trophy Cup (floral design), 1914
Thrown by Elizabeth Gray Overbeck
Decorated by Mary Frances Overbeck
Stoneware
H. 14 in.; Dia. 6⅞ in.
Marks: under base, incised conjoined ciphers of *OBK*
and *EF*
Los Angeles County Museum of Art; Gift of Max
Palevsky and Jodie Evans in honor of the museum's
twenty-fifth anniversary (M.89.151.16)
(p. 154)

Vase (nasturtium design), 1915
Thrown by Elizabeth Gray Overbeck
Decorated by Mary Frances Overbeck
Earthenware
H. 18 in.; Dia. 8 in.
Marks: under base, incised conjoined ciphers of *OBK*
and *E F*
Overbeck Pottery Room, Cambridge City Public
Library; Postle Collection (F-2)
(p. 155)

Vase, ca. 1915
Thrown by Elizabeth Gray Overbeck
Decorated by Mary Frances Overbeck
Earthenware
H. 12¼ in.; Dia. 5 in.
Marks: impressed on bottom, ciphers of *OBK* and *E F*
Indianapolis Museum of Art; Gift of the Indiana
Chapter of the Society of Western Artists (17.247)
(p. 156)

Vase (gingko-leaf and deer design), n.d.
Thrown by Elizabeth Gray Overbeck
Decorated by Mary Frances Overbeck
Earthenware
H. 12 in.; Dia. 7 in.
Marks: impressed ciphers of *OBK* and *E F*
Richmond Art Museum (72.5)
(p. 157)

Vase (windblown-tree design), n.d.
Thrown by Elizabeth Gray Overbeck
Decorated by Mary Frances Overbeck
Earthenware
H. 15½ in.; Dia. 8 in.
Marks: impressed ciphers of *OBK* and *E F*
Richmond Art Museum (44.9.1)
(p. 158)

Vase (figurative design), n.d.
Thrown by Elizabeth Gray Overbeck
Decorated by Mary Frances Overbeck
Earthenware
H. 12 in.; Dia. 5½ in.
Marks: under base, incised conjoined ciphers of *OBK*
and *E F*
Overbeck Pottery Room, Cambridge City Public
Library, Postle Collection (F-12)
(p. 159)

HANNAH BORGER OVERBECK
(American, 1870–1931)

Fuchsias, from the *Overbeck Sketchbook*, ca. 1915
Watercolor
H. 8⁵⁄₁₆ in.; W. 11¼ in.
Los Angeles County Museum of Art; Museum
Acquisitions Fund (M.88.35.3.1-.29)
(p. 190)

Bowl, "Farewell Summer Design," ca. 1915
Watercolor and pastel
H. 4 in.; W. 10⅛ in.
Los Angeles Country Museum of Art: Museum
Acquisitions Fund (M.88.35.3.7)
(p. 190)

MARGARET JORDAN PATTERSON
(American, born in Indonesia, 1867–1950)

Summer Clouds, ca. 1918
Color woodcut
H. 11⅜ in.; W. 9 in.
Private collection
(p. 40)

In the High Hills, ca. 1925
Color woodcut
H. 11¼ in.; W. 8⅞ in.
Collection Leslie and Joanna Garfield
(p. 41)

PEWABIC POTTERY (Detroit, 1903–1961)

Plate, ca. 1905
Earthenware
Dia. 12 in.
Marks: *Pewabic*
Collection Stephen Gray
(p. 160)

WILBUR HEBER PORTERFIELD
(American, 1873–1958)

Trees of Lombardy, 1903
Carbon print
H. 16 in.; W. 20 in.
Benjamans Art Gallery, Buffalo, New York
(p. 98)

PAUL REVERE POTTERY OF THE SATURDAY
EVENING GIRLS' CLUB (Boston, 1906–1942)

Vase, ca. 1912
Decorated by Albina Mangini
Earthenware
H. 6¼ in.; Dia. 4 in.
Marks: on back, impressed *S.E.G. 12-17 by AM*
Private collection
(p. 161)

WILLIAM S. RICE (American, 1873–1963)

Marsh Moon, ca. 1925
Color woodcut
H. 9⅜ in.; W. 10¾ in.
Worcester Art Museum, Worcester, Massachusetts;
Anonymous gift (1988.82)
(p. 42)

Block Prints: How to Make Them
Milwaukee: The Bruce Publishing Company, 1941
H. 10¼ in.; W. 7½ in.; D. ⅝ in.
Private collection
(p. 191)

ADELAIDE ALSOP ROBINEAU
(American, 1865–1929)

Vase (Viking-ship design), 1905
Porcelain
H. 7¼ in.; Dia. 2¾ in.
Marks: under base, excised cipher of conjoined *A R*
in a circle; incised *570*; on inside of ring base, in a
rectangle, incised cipher of conjoined *A R*
Everson Museum of Art (16.4.1 a–b)
(p. 162)

Lantern, 1908
Porcelain
H. 8 in.; Dia. 6 in.
Marks: on inside, incised cipher of conjoined *A R;
1908; 668*
Everson Museum of Art (16.4.5)
(p. 163)

Vase (scarab design), before 1917
Porcelain
H. 12 in.; Dia. 4 in.
Marks: under base, in a circle, excised cipher of
conjoined *A R*; incised *506*
Everson Museum of Art (16.4.32)
(p. 164)

CHARLES ROHLFS (American, 1853–1936)

Frame (tree design), 1902
American white oak
H. 26 in.; W. 26 in.; D. ⅝ in.
Collection David Cathers
(p. 192)

RUDOLPH SCHAEFFER (American, 1886–1988)

Tray, 1912
Copper
Dia. 13½ in.
Oakland Museum of California; Gift of the Estate of
Rudolph Schaeffer (A88.59.2)
(p. 193)

WILHELMINA SEEGMILLER
(American, 1866–1913)

Flower Study, ca. 1908
Color woodcut
H. 7½ in.; W. 11¹³⁄₁₆ in.
Indianapolis Museum of Art; Gift of Mary E. Nicholson
(17.51)
(p. 43)

Flower Study, 1908
Color woodcut
H. 11⁵⁄₁₆ in.; W. 7⅝ in.
Indianapolis Museum of Art; Gift of Mary E. Nicholson
(17.52)
(p. 44)

ANNA FRANCES SIMPSON (American, 1880–1930)

Table Runner, n.d.
Linen and silk
L. 63½ in.; W. 16 in.
Museum of Art, Rhode Island School of Design; Gift of
Mrs. Eliot A. Carver (1991.114.1)
(p. 194)

ALICE RAVENEL HUGER SMITH
(American, 1876–1958)

Moon Flower and Hawk Moth, 1918
Color woodcut
H. 9 in.; W. 8 in.
Gibbes Museum of Art, Charleston; Gift of
Mrs. W.E. Simms (62.02.58.01)
(p. 45)

Untitled (trees with moss and moon), n.d.
Color woodcut
H. 11½ in.; W. 8⅜ in.
Gibbes Museum of Art, Charleston; Gift of
Mrs. W.E. Simms (62.02.46)
(p. 46)

PAMELA COLMAN SMITH (American, 1878–1951)
AND JACK BUTLER YEATS (Irish, 1871–1957)

A Broad Sheet, June 1902
Hand-colored illustrations; poem by A.E.
H. 19⅞ in.; W. 15 in.
Museum of Fine Arts, Boston; Gift of Miss Mildred
Howells (50.2837)
(p. 195)

A Broad Sheet, August 1902
Hand-colored illustrations; poems by Anon and
W.W. Gibson
H. 19⅞ in.; W. 15 in.
Museum of Fine Arts, Boston; Gift of Miss Mildred
Howells (50.2839)
(p. 196)

ZULMA STEELE (American, 1881–1979)

Sheet of Plant Studies and Border Designs, ca. 1910
Pencil and watercolor
H. 23 in.; W. 17 in.
Collection Jean and Jim Young
(p. 47)

The High Mountain, ca. 1910–14
Monotype
H. 8 in.; W. 9¾ in.
Collection Jean and Jim Young
(p. 48)

Fourth of July, ca. 1920
Watercolor and crayon
Each, H. 10¾ in.; W. 2 in.
Collection Jean and Jim Young
(p. 49)

EDWARD STEICHEN
(American, born in Luxembourg, 1879–1973)

Landscape, ca. 1897
Platinum print
H. 9½ in.; W. 7⅜ in.
George Eastman House, Rochester, New York; Bequest
of Edward Steichen (79:2011:1)
Reproduced with permission of Joanna T. Steichen
(p. 99)

Moonlight, The Pond, 1906
Photogravure
H. 6⅜ in.; W. 8 in.
Crocker Art Museum; Gift of Graham Nash (1980.14)
(p. 100)

ALFRED STIEGLITZ (American, 1864–1946)

Spring Showers, 1900 (printed ca. 1913)
Photogravure
H. 12¼ in.; W. 5 in.
The Metropolitan Museum of Art; The Alfred Stieglitz
Collection, 1949 (49.55.14)
(p. 101)

Dancing Trees, 1921–22
Palladium print
H. 9½ in.; W. 7⅝ in.
The Metropolitan Museum of Art; Gift of David A.
Schulte, 1928 (28.127.7)
(p. 102)

M. LOUISE STOWELL (American, 1861–1930)

Untitled (Ipswich Bridge), 1892
Watercolor
H. 16 in.; W. 12 in.
Strong Museum, Rochester, New York (73.2341)
(p. 50)

Untitled (summer landscape), 1892
Watercolor, pen, and ink
H. 10⅞ in.; W. 13¾ in.
Strong Museum, Rochester, New York (73.2342)
(p. 51)

KARL STRUSS (American, 1886–1981)

Tree in Landscape, 1909
Platinum print
H. 9¼ in.; W. 7 in.
The Metropolitan Museum of Art; Purchase, Warner
Communications, Inc., and Matching Funds from the
National Endowment for the Arts, 1980 (1980.1012)
(p. 103)

Avenue of Pines, 1909
Palladium print
H. 9 in.; W. 7 in.
Herbert F. Johnson Museum of Art, Cornell University;
Bequest of William P. Chapman, Jr., Class of 1895
(62.3302)
(p. 103)

In the Southland: Mt. Baldy, California, ca. 1921
Gum platinum print
H. 13 in.; W. 10 in.
Oakland Museum of California; Gift of Mr. and Mrs.
Willard M. Knott (A82.7)
(p. 104)

AUGUSTUS THIBAUDEAU (American, 1866–1939)

Lonely Pine Tree, ca. 1908
Platinum print
H. 13⁹⁄₁₆ in.; W. 9¹¹⁄₁₆ in.
Albright-Knox Art Gallery, Buffalo, New York; Gift of
Marie Thibaudeau (P1979:29.4)
(p. 105)

Lily Pad in Reflecting Pond, ca. 1910
Platinum print
H. 13¼ in.; W. 10 in.
Castellani Art Museum, Niagara University; Gift of Miss
Marie Thibaudeau, 1979 (NU07179)
(p. 105)

VOLKMAR KILNS (Metuchen, New Jersey, 1902–1911)

Tile (birch-tree design), ca. 1910
Earthenware
H. 8 in.; W. 8 in.; D. ¾ in.
Marks: on face, *V*; on back, stamped in ink *VOLKMAR
KILNS/METUCHEN, N. J.*
The Newark Museum; Gift of William B. Kinny, 1911
(11.466)
(p. 165)

WALRATH POTTERY
(Rochester, New York, 1908–1918)

Vase (pine-cone design), 1908–18
Earthenware
H. 8¼ in.; Dia. 4½ in.
Marks: none
Collection Alexandra Sheldon
(p. 166)

Vase (floral design), ca. 1910
Earthenware
H. 8½ in.; Dia. 3¼ in.
Marks: *Walrath Pottery/MI* I
Buffalo and Erie County Historical Society (65-1337r)
(p. 167)

Vase (iris design), ca. 1910
Stoneware
H. 19 in.; Dia. 3⅝ in.
Marks: incised *Walrath Pottery*; incised *MI* cipher
The Newark Museum; Purchase 1911 (11.505)
(p. 168)

MAX WEBER (American, born in Russia, 1881–1961)

Paris Rooftops (Cityscape), 1906
Monotype
H. 3⅝ in.; W. 5⅛ in.
Courtesy Forum Gallery, New York
(FO12886)
(p. 52)

Woman Seated at a Table, ca. 1920
Color woodcut
H. 4⅛ in.; W. 1⅞ in.
Courtesy Forum Gallery, New York
(FO10235)
(p. 53)

CLARENCE H. WHITE (American, 1871–1925)

Telegraph Poles, 1898
Platinum print
H. 13½ in.; W. 8 in.
Licking County Historical Society, Newark, Ohio
(DAM#3)
(p. 106)

Woodland Scene, ca. 1905
Gum bichromate print
H. 7¾ in.; W. 6 in.
Licking County Historical Society, Newark, Ohio
(p. 107)

ARTISTS UNKNOWN

Wall Hanging (sunlit bayou), ca. 1902–15
Linen with silk thread
H. 16¼ in.; W. 45 in.
H. Sophie Newcomb College, Tulane University
(p. 197)

Table Runner (pine-tree design), ca. 1905–15
Linen with silk thread
L. 64 in.; W. 16¼ in.
H. Sophie Newcomb College, Tulane University; Gift of
Mrs. Felice Maurer Lowe
(p. 198)

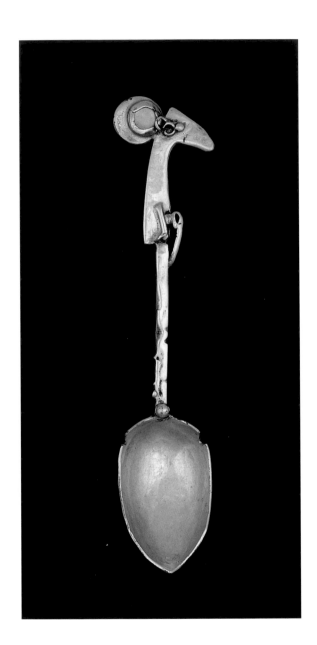

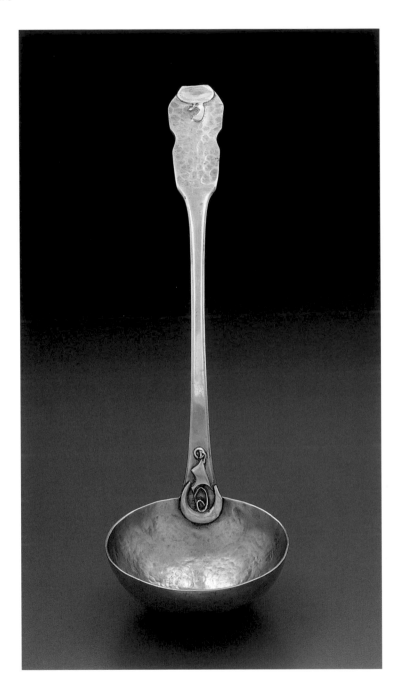

JANET PAYNE BOWLES
Spoon, ca. 1912–15

JANET PAYNE BOWLES
Ladle, ca. 1916–19

BYRDCLIFFE COLONY
Linen Press, ca. 1904

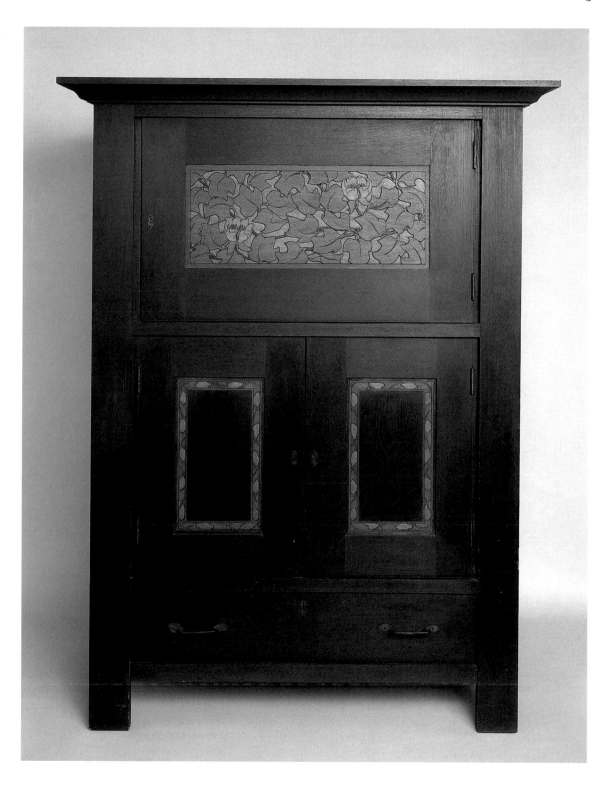

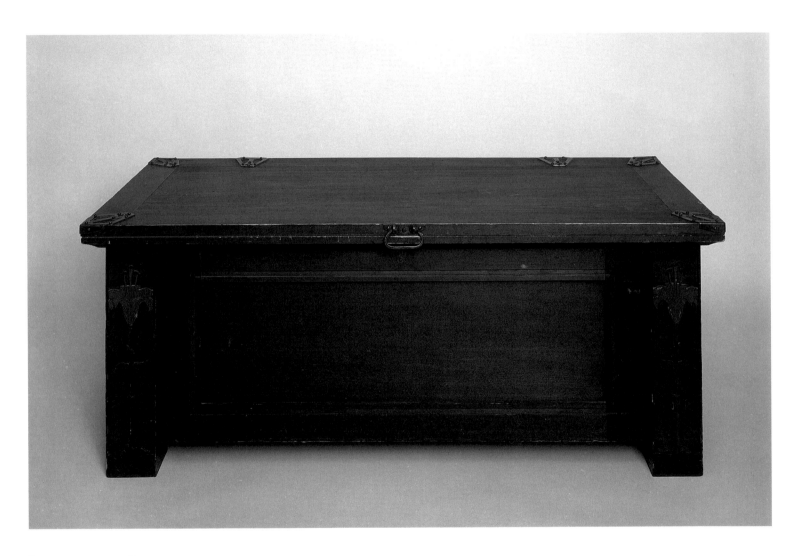

BYRDCLIFFE COLONY
Chest, ca. 1904

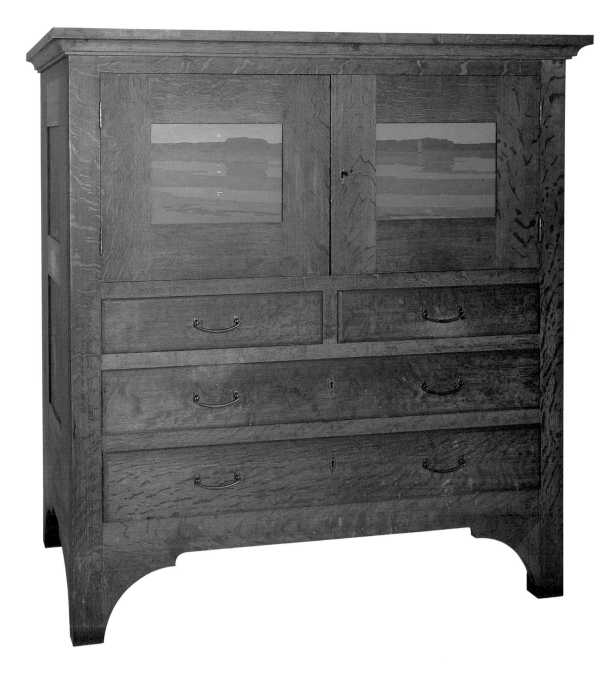

Byrdcliffe Colony
Chest, ca. 1904

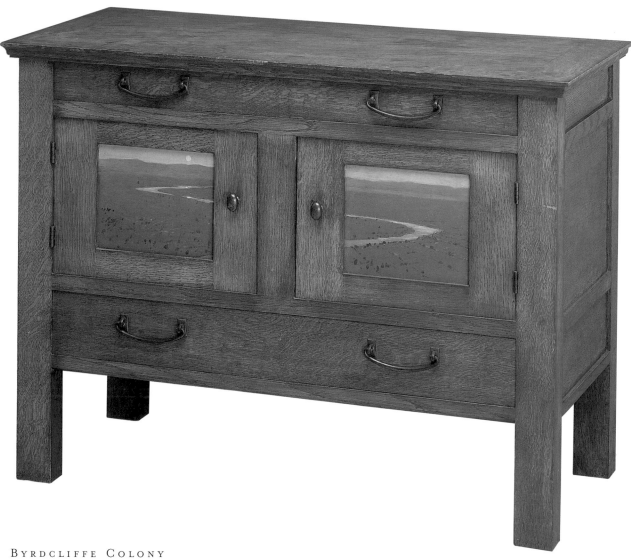

Byrdcliffe Colony
Cabinet, ca. 1904

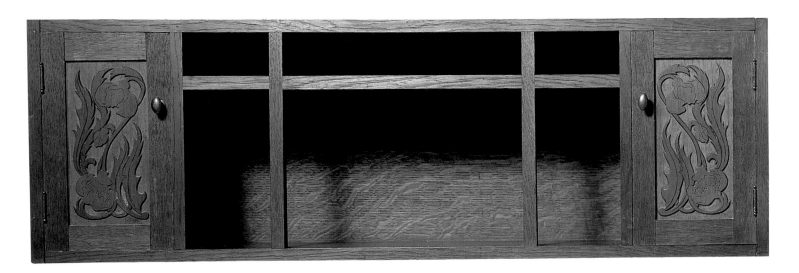

BYRDCLIFFE COLONY
Hanging Cabinet, n.d.

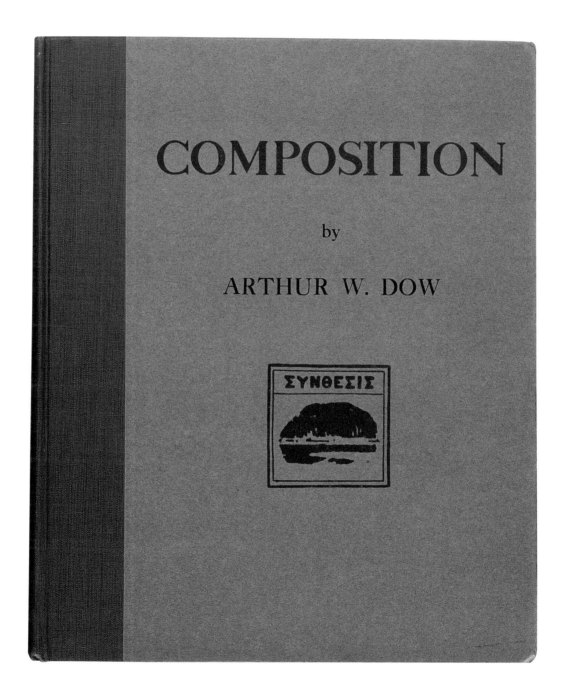

ARTHUR WESLEY DOW
Composition: A Series of Exercises in Art Structure for the Use of
Students and Teachers, 1913

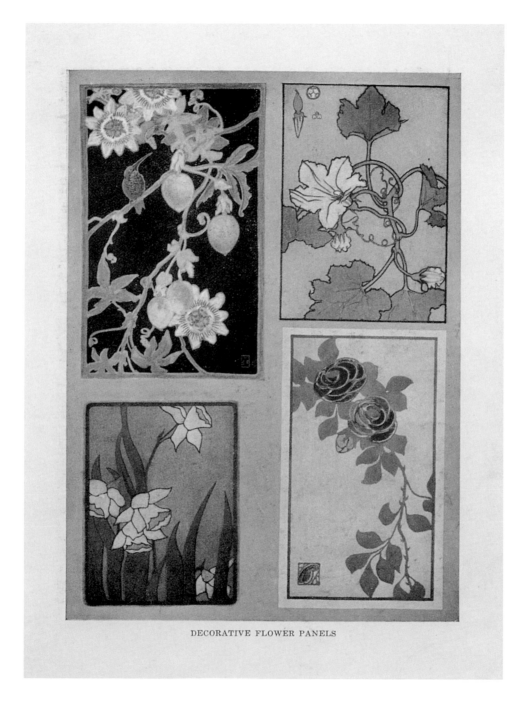

DECORATIVE FLOWER PANELS

PEDRO DE LEMOS
Page from *The Art Teacher: A Book for Children and Teachers,* 1949

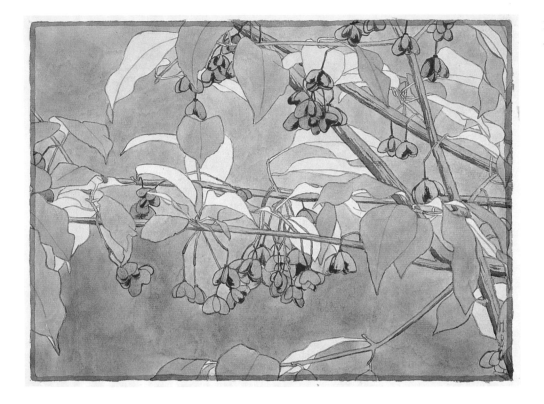

HANNAH BORGER OVERBECK
Fuchsias, from the *Overbeck Sketchbook*, ca. 1915

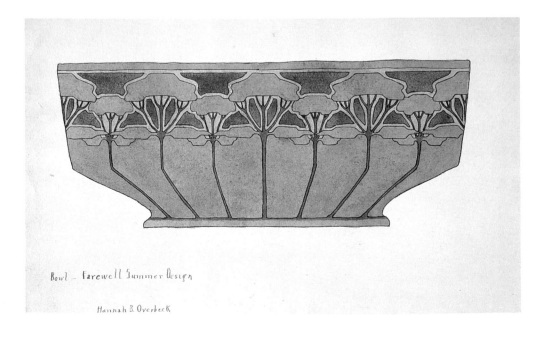

HANNAH BORGER OVERBECK
Bowl, "Farewell Summer Design," ca. 1915

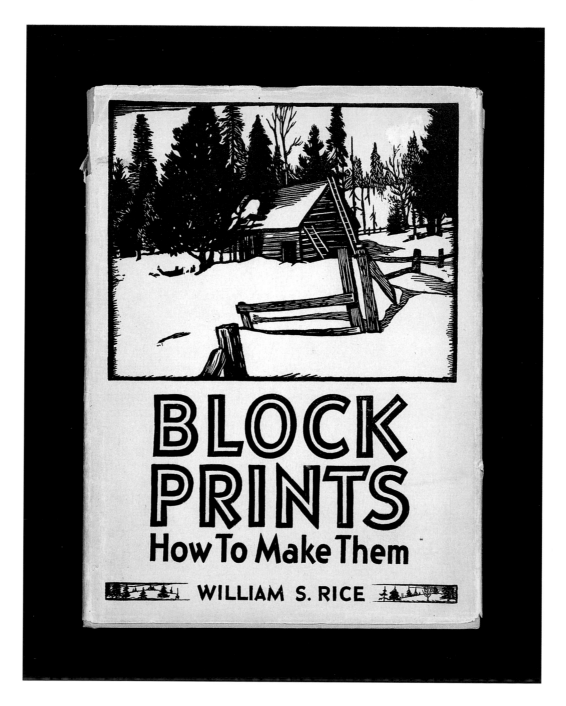

WILLIAM S. RICE
Block Prints: How to Make Them, 1941

CHARLES ROHLFS
Frame (tree design), 1902

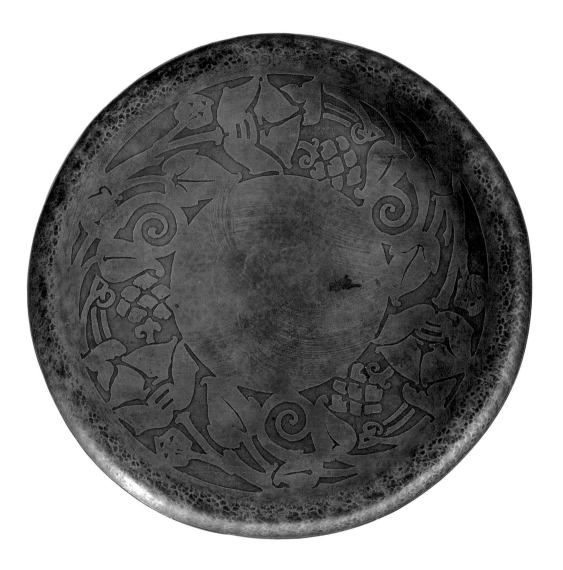

Rudolph Schaeffer
Tray, 1912

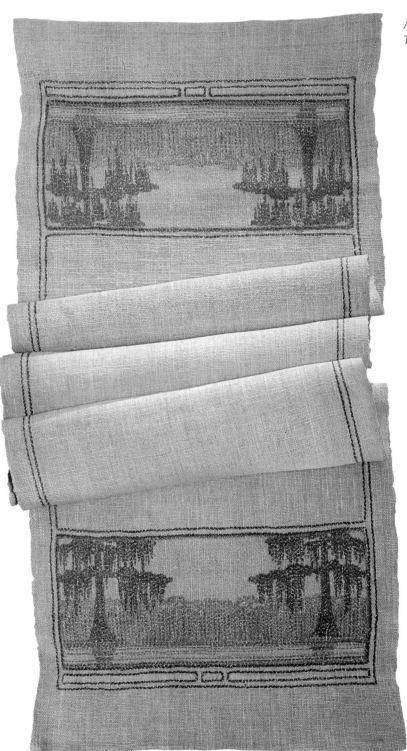

ANNA FRANCES SIMPSON
Table Runner, n.d.

A BROAD SHEET

JUNE, 1902

PICTURES BY MISS PAMELA COLMAN SMITH AND JACK B. YEATS.

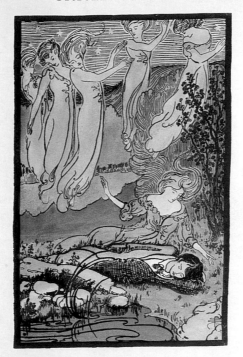

THE GATES OF DREAMLAND.

It's a lonely road through bogland to the lake at Carrowmore,
And a sleeper there lies dreaming, where the water laps the shore.
Though the moth wings of the twilight in their purples are unfurled,
Yet his sleep is filled with music by the masters of the world.

There's a hand is white as silver that is fondling with his hair,
There are glimmering feet of sunshine that are dancing by him there,
And half open lips of faery that were dyed to richest red
In their revels where the Hazel Tree its holy clusters shed.

"Come away," the red lips whisper, "all the world is weary now,
'Tis the twilight of the ages, and it's time to quit the plough.
Oh, the very sunlight's weary ere it lightens up the dew,
And its gold is changed to grey light before it falls to you."

"Though your colleen's heart is tender, a tenderer heart is near;
What's the starlight in her glances when the stars are shining clear?
Who would kiss the fading shadow, when the flower face glows above?
'Tis the Beauty of all Beauty that is calling for your love."

Oh, the mountain gates of dreamland have opened once again,
And the sound of song and dancing falls upon the ears of men;
And the Land of Youth lies gleaming, lit with rainbow light and mirth,
And the old enchantment lingers in the honey heart of earth.

A. E.

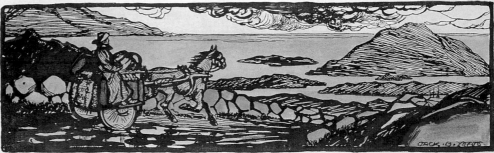

THE MAIL CAR.

Hand coloured. Post free. 12 Shillings a Year. In America, 3 Dollars a Year. A Specimen Copy may be had 13 Pence, post free.

PUBLISHED AND SOLD BY ELKIN MATHEWS, VIGO STREET, LONDON, W.

No. 6   All Rights Reserved

FARNCOMBE & SON, PRINTERS, CROYDON

PAMELA COLMAN SMITH
AND JACK BUTLER YEATS
A Broad Sheet, June 1902

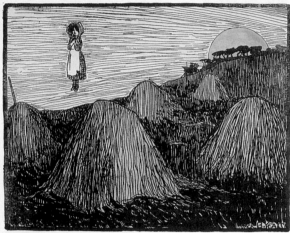

A BROAD SHEET

AUGUST, 1902

PICTURES BY PAMELA COLMAN SMITH AND JACK B. YEATS.

LITTLE LIZA.

Don't you hear me callin', callin' at the fallin' of the May?
I'm the ghost of little Liza, as was smothered in the hay.

✦ ✦ ✦ ✦ ✦

For it fell upon a Sunday, just about this time of day,
I went out with lots of others for to romp among the hay.
We was happy, oh! so happy, we did run and screech and shout,
And we clapper-clawed each other as we flung the hay about.
There was me and Cousin Minnie as was running after Jim,
When he fell across a furrow, and I fell on top of him,
And they heaped a haycock on us; Jim, he was rumbusticall;
Out he wriggled, but I couldn't, cause you see I was so small,
And they never thought of Liza as they laughed and tore away,
Never thought of little Liza, as was buried in the hay.
It was just as if a mountain had a fell atop my head,
First I tried to kick and struggle, then I tried to scream instead,
Then at last I grew quite quiet, and a stunning, buzzing sound
Filled my ears, 'twas just as if the field was going round and
   round.
All that night, and early Monday, underneath the pook I lay,
Until father came next morning for to stackle up the hay.
Father'd been abed all Sunday, tired with mowing of the grass,
And I hadn't got no mammy for to wonder where I was.
Then the man as was a tossing of the cocks into the cart,
Sticks his pitchfork in my pinny, then he stops and gives a start,
But he didn't go to hurt me, an' you musn't think he did,
Even father never wondered where his little girl was hid.
So they drove me to the village, with my Sunday pinny torn,
Stretched upon the big hay waggon—dead, against the rising
   morn,
And the clergyman next Sunday told of where all hurts are
   healed,
An' he buried me for nothink, 'cause he said it was *his* field.

✦ ✦ ✦ ✦ ✦

Don't you hear me callin', callin' at the fallin' of the May?
I'm the ghost of little Liza, as was smothered in the hay.
                   ANON

By permission of the Editors of "Longman's Magazine."

THE MOUNTAIN LOVERS.

Was it for this we loved, O Time, to be
Among Love's deathless through eternity,
Set high on lone divided peaks above,
The sheltered summer valley spreads between?
Was it for this our joy, our grief has been,
Our barren daydreams, dream-deserted nights,
That valley lovers, looking up, might see
How vain is Love among the starry heights,
And loving sigh, "How vain a thing is love"?

O Love, that we had found thee in the shade,
Where all day long the deep leaf-hidden glade
Hears but the moan of some forsaken dove,
Or the clear song of happy nameless streams,
Where all night long the August moonlight gleams
Through warm green dusk, no longer cold and white;
O Love, that we had found thee unafraid
One summer morn and followed thee till night,
As unknown valley lovers follow Love.

      WILFRID WILSON GIBSON.

PAMELA COLMAN SMITH
AND JACK BUTLER YEATS
A Broad Sheet, August 1902

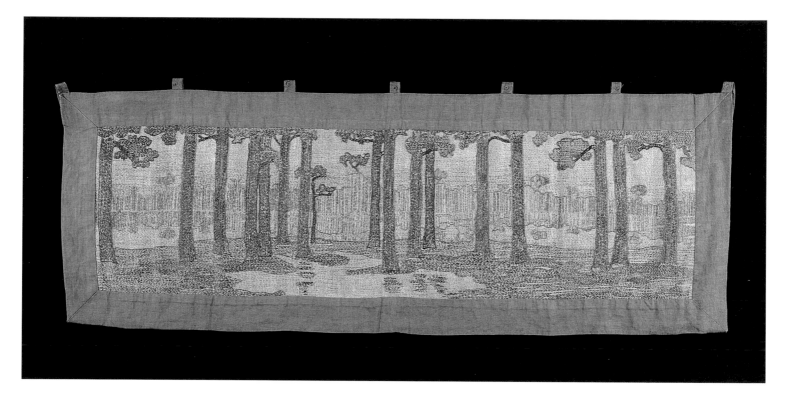

Artist Unknown
Wall Hanging (sunlit bayou), ca. 1902–15

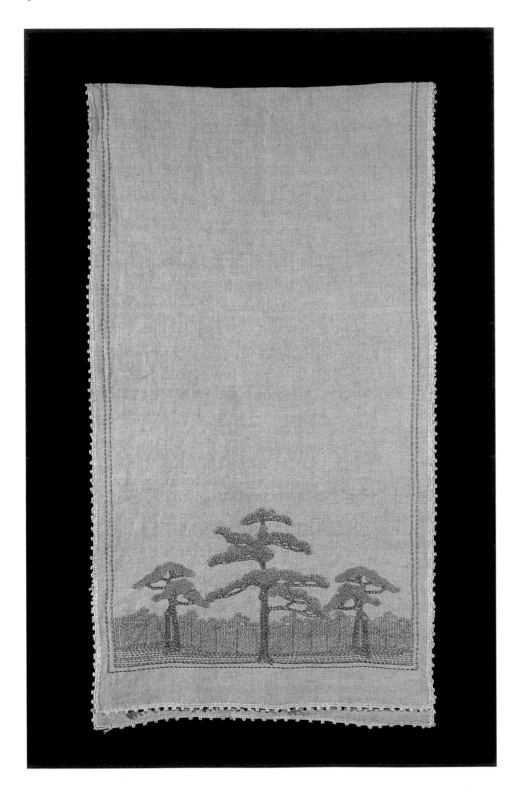

ARTIST UNKNOWN
Table Runner (pine-tree design), ca. 1905–15

SELECTED BIBLIOGRAPHY

Acton, David. *A Spectrum of Innovation: Color in American Printmaking, 1890–1960.* New York: W. W. Norton & Company, 1990.

Adams, Clinton. *Crayonstone: The Life and Work of Bolton Brown.* Albuquerque: University of New Mexico Press, 1993.

Adams, Clinton, ed. *Second Impressions: Modern Prints and Printmakers Reconsidered.* Albuquerque: University of New Mexico Press, 1996.

Austin, Bruce A. *The American Arts & Crafts Movement in Western New York, 1900–1920.* Rochester: Bruce A. Austin, 1992.

Bannon, Anthony. *The Photo-Pictorialists of Buffalo.* Buffalo: Media Studio, 1981.

Baxter, Sylvester. "Handicraft, and Its Extension at Ipswich." *Handicraft* 1, no. 11 (February 1903): 249–68.

Berger, Klaus. *Japonisme in Western Painting from Whistler to Matisse.* Cambridge: Cambridge University Press, 1980.

Boruff, Blanche Foster, comp. *Women of Indiana.* Indianapolis: Indiana Women's Biography Association, Indianapolis, 1986.

Boswell, Peyton. "The New American School of Wood Block Printers in Color." *Art World* 9 (July 1918): 168–69, 188.

Bothwell, Dora, and Marlys Frey. *Notan.* New York: Reinhold Book Corp., 1968.

Bowman, Leslie Greene. *American Arts and Crafts: Virtue in Design.* Los Angeles: Los Angeles County Museum of Art in association with Bulfinch Press/Little, Brown and Company, 1990.

Brooks, Van Wyck. *Fenollosa and His Circle.* New York: E. P. Dutton & Co., 1962.

Brown, Lucy. "The First Summer in Byrdcliffe." *Publications of the Woodstock Historical Society* 13 (August–September 1937): 3–14.

Bry, Doris. *Alfred Stieglitz.* Washington, D.C.: National Gallery of Art, 1958.

Bunnell, Peter, ed. *A Photographic Vision: Pictorial Photography, 1889–1923.* Salt Lake City: Peregrine Smith, Inc., 1980.

Caffin, Charles. *Photography As a Fine Art.* New York: Doubleday, Page & Co., 1901.

Carney, Margaret. *Charles Fergus Binns: The Father of American Studio Ceramics.* New York: Hudson Hills Press, Inc. 1998.

Clark, Robert Judson, ed. *The Arts and Crafts Movement in America, 1876–1916.* Princeton: Princeton University Press, 1972.

Colby, Joy Hakanson. *Arts and Crafts in Detroit, 1906–1976.* Detroit: Detroit Institute of Art, 1976.

Coles, William A. *Herman Dudley Murphy: "Realism Married to Idealism Most Exquisitely."* New York: Graham Galleries, 1982.

Corn, Wanda M. *The Color of Mood: American Tonalism, 1880–1910.* San Francisco: M. H. de Young Memorial Museum and the California Palace of the Legion of Honor, 1972.

Cox, George. "The Horizon of A. W. Dow." *International Studio* 77, no. 313 (June 1923): 189–93.

Dietz, Ulysses G. *The Newark Museum Collection of American Pottery.* Salt Lake City: Gibbs M. Smith, 1984.

Dow, Arthur Wesley. "Printing from Wooden Blocks." *International Studio* 59 (July 1916): xv–xvi.

———. "Talks on Appreciation of Art." *The Delineator* (January 1915): 15; (February 1915): 15; (April 1915): 15; (July 1915): 15.

———. *Theory and Practice of Teaching Art.* New York: Teachers College Columbia University, 1908.

————. "Appreciation." *Pratt Institute Monthly* 7, no. 3 (January 1899): 69–72.

————. *Composition: A Series of Exercises in Art Structure for the Use of Students and Teachers.* 1899. Reprint, New York: Doubleday, Page and Co., Inc., 1913. Reprint, Berkeley: University of California Press, 1997. Introduction by Joseph Masheck.

————. "Painting with Wooden Blocks." *Modern Art* 4 (Summer 1896): 85–90.

————. "A Note on a New System of Art-Teaching." *Pratt Institute Monthly* 5, no. 4 (December 1896): 92.

————. "A Note on Japanese Art and What the American Artist May Learn Therefrom." *Knight Errant* (January 1893): 114–16.

Edwards, Robert, and Jane Perkins Claney. *Life by Design: The Byrdcliffe Arts and Crafts Colony.* Wilmington: Delaware Art Museum, 1984.

Edwards, Robert. "The Utopias of Ralph Radcliffe Whitehead." *Antiques* 127, no. 1 (January 1985): 260–75

Evans, Paul. *Art Pottery of the United States.* New York: Feingold & Lewis Publishing, 1987.

Evers, Alf. *Woodstock: History of an American Town.* Woodstock, N.Y.: Overlook Press, 1987.

————. *The Catskills: From Wilderness to Woodstock.* Garden City, N.Y.: Doubleday & Company, 1972.

Fenollosa, Ernest F. *Epochs of Chinese and Japanese Art,* 2 vols. London: William Heinemann, 1912.

————. "Arthur W. Dow," *The Lotos* 9 (March 1896): 709–10.

Fidler, Patricia. *Art with a Mission: Objects of the Arts and Crafts Movement.* Lawrence, Kan.: Spencer Museum of Art, 1991.

Finlay, Nancy. *Artists of the Book in Boston, 1890–1910* Boston: Houghton Library, 1985.

Flint, Janet. *Provincetown Printers: A Woodcut Tradition.* Washington, D.C.: Smithsonian Institution Press, 1983.

Fulton, Marianne, ed. *Pictorialism into Modernism: The Clarence H. White School of Photography.* New York: Rizzoli, 1996.

Garb, Tamar. *Sisters of the Brush: Women's Artistic Culture in Late Nineteenth-Century Paris.* New Haven: Yale University Press, 1994.

Goodrich, Lloyd. *Max Weber.* New York: Whitney Museum of American Art, 1949.

Goodrich, Lloyd, and Doris Bry. *Georgia O'Keeffe.* New York: Whitney Museum of American Art, 1970.

Gravulos, Mary Evans O'Keefe, and Carol Pulin. *Bertha Lum.* Washington, D.C.: Smithsonian Institution Press, 1991.

Green, Nancy E. *Arthur Wesley Dow and His Influence.* Ithaca, N.Y.: Herbert F. Johnson Museum of Art, 1990.

Hartmann, Sadakichi. *Japanese Art.* Boston: L. C. Page and Co., 1903.

Hawes, Lloyd E. *The Dedham Pottery and the Earlier Robertson's Chelsea Potteries.* Dedham, Mass.: Dedham Historical Society, 1968.

Hoeber, Arthur. *Catalogue of an Exhibition of Paintings by Alexander Harrison and Birge Harrison.* Chicago: Chicago Art Institute, 1913.

Homer, William Innes. *Alfred Stieglitz and the American Avant-Garde.* Boston: New York Graphic Society, 1977.

————. et al. *A Pictorial Heritage: The Photographs of Gertrude Käsebier.* Wilmington: Delaware Art Museum, 1979.

————. ed. *Pictorial Photography in Philadelphia: The Pennsylvania Academy's Salons, 1898–1901.* Philadelphia: Pennsylvania Academy of the Fine Arts, 1984.

Howard, Blanche Willis. *Guenn, A Wave on the Breton Coast.* Boston: James R. Osgood and Co., 1883.

Hughes, Edan Milton. *Artists in California, 1786–1940.* Ann Arbor, Mich.: Braun-Brumfield, 1989.

Johnson, Arthur Warren. *Arthur Wesley Dow: Historian, Artist, Teacher.* Ipswich, Mass.: Ipswich Historical Society, 1934.

Jones, Harvey. *Mathews: Masterpieces of the California Decorative Style.* Oakland, Calif.: Oakland Museum, 1985.

Kaplan, Wendy. *The Art That Is Life: The Arts and Crafts Movement in America, 1875–1920.* Boston: Museum of Fine Arts, 1987.

Kardon, Janet, ed. *The Ideal Home: The History of Twentieth-Century American Craft, 1900–1920.* New York: Harry N. Abrams, 1993.

Keen, Kirsten Hoving. *American Art Pottery, 1875–1930.* Wilmington: Delaware Art Museum, 1978.

Key, Mabel. "A New System of Art Education, Arranged and Directed by Arthur W. Dow." *Brush and Pencil* 4 (August 1899): 258–70.

Kingsley, April. "Women Artists at the Frontiers of Modernism." *Provincetown Arts* (1988): 68– 71, 169–70.

Koehler, S. R., ed. "Japanese Wood-Cutting and Wood-Cut Printing." *Report of the U. S. National Museum.* Washington, D.C.: Government Printing Office, 1893.

Kuh, Katherine, ed. *The Artist's Voice.* New York: Harper and Row, 1962.

Longwell, Dennis. *Steichen: The Master Prints, 1895–1914.* Boston: New York Graphic Society, 1978.

Ludwig, Coy L. *The Arts and Crafts Movement in New York State, 1890s–1920s.* Hamilton, N.Y.: Gallery Association of New York State, 1983.

Lynes, Barbara Buhler. *O'Keeffe, Stieglitz and the Critics, 1916– 1929.* Chicago: University of Chicago Press, 1989.

McCandless, Barbara, Bonnie Yochelson, and Richard Koszarski. *New York to Hollywood: The Photography of Karl Struss.* Albuquerque: University of New Mexico Press, 1995.

Meech, Julia, and Gabriel P. Weisberg. *Japonisme Comes to America.* New York: Harry N. Abrams, 1990.

Meyer, Marilee Boyd, et al. *Inspiring Reform: Boston's Arts and Crafts Movement.* Wellesley, Mass.: Davis Museum and Cultural Center, in association with Bulfinch Press/ Little, Brown and Company, 1997.

Michaels, Barbara L. *Gertrude Käsebier.* New York: Harry N. Abrams, 1992.

Mills, Sally. *Japanese Influences in American Art, 1853–1900.* Williamstown, Mass.: Sterling and Francine Clark Art Institute, 1981.

Moffatt, Frederick C. *Arthur Wesley Dow, 1857–1922.* Washington D.C.: Smithsonian Institution Press, 1977.

Montgomery, Susan J. *The Ceramics of William H. Grueby.* Lambertville, N.J.: Arts & Crafts Quarterly Press, 1993.

Moore, Eudorah M., et al. *California Design 1910.* Pasadena Center: California Design Publications, 1974.

Morrell, Dora. "Hermann Dudley Murphy." *Brush and Pencil* 5, no. 2 (November 1899): 49–57.

Munro, Thomas. "The Dow Method and Public School Art." *Journal of the Barnes Foundation* 12 (January 1926): 35–40.

Ormond, Suzanne, and Mary E. Irvine. *Louisiana's Art Nouveau.* Gretna, La.: Pelican Publishing Company, 1976.

Parsons, Melinda Boyd. *To All Believers: The Art of Pamela Colman Smith.* Wilmington: Delaware Art Museum, 1975.

Peters, Sarah Whitaker. *Becoming O'Keeffe: The Early Years.* New York: Abbeville Press, 1991.

Peterson, Christian A. "The Photograph Beautiful, 1895– 1915," *History of Photography* 16, no. 3 (Autumn 1992): 189–232.

Pisano, Ronald G. *One Hundred Years: A Centennial Celebration of the National Association of Women Artists.* Roslyn Harbor, N.Y.: Nassau County Museum of Fine Art, 1988.

Poesch, Jessie. *Newcomb Pottery: An Enterprise for Southern Women, 1895–1940.* West Chester, Penn.: Schiffer Publishing Limited, 1984.

Postle, Kathleen. *The Chronicle of the Overbeck Pottery.* Indianapolis: Indianapolis Historical Society, 1978.

Pollitzer, Anita. *A Woman on Paper: Georgia O'Keeffe.* New York: Simon & Schuster, 1988.

Priestman, Mabel Tuke. "History of the Arts and Crafts Movement in America." *House Beautiful* 20 (October 1906): 15–16; (November 1906): 14–16.

Ross, Denman Waldo. *On Drawing and Painting.* Boston: Houghton Mifflin Company, 1912.

———. *A Theory of Pure Design.* Boston: Houghton Mifflin Company, 1907.

———. "The Arts and Crafts: A Diagnosis." *Handicraft* 1, no. 10 (January 1903): 229–43.

Shifman, Barry. *The Arts & Crafts Metalwork of Janet Payne Bowles.* Indianapolis: Indianapolis Museum of Art, 1993.

Smith, Katherine Louise. "Women in the Arts and Crafts." *Brush and Pencil* 5 (November 1899): 76–79.

Spain, May R. *The Society of Arts and Crafts.* Boston: Society of Arts and Crafts, 1924.

Staley, Alan. "Byrdcliffe and the Maverick." M.A. Thesis, Yale University, 1960.

Story, Ala. *Max Weber.* University of California, Santa Barbara, 1968.

Thompson, Bertha. "The Craftsmen at Byrdcliffe." *Publications of the Woodstock Historical Society* 10 (July 1933): 8–13.

Trapp, Kenneth R., et al. *The Arts and Crafts Movement in California: Living the Good Life.* New York: Abbeville Press, 1993.

———. *American Art Pottery.* New York: Cooper-Hewitt Museum, 1987.

Weaver, Jane Calhoun, ed. *Sadakichi Hartmann: Critical Modernist.* Berkeley: University of California Press, 1991.

Weaver, Mike. "The Japanese Influence." *Aperture,* no. 104 (Fall 1986): 11–21.

Weiss, Peg, ed. *Adelaide Alsop Robineau: Glory in Porcelain.* Syracuse, N.Y.: Syracuse University Press, 1981.

Whelan, Richard. *Alfred Stieglitz: A Biography.* New York: Da Capo Press, 1997.

White, Maynard. *Clarence H. White.* New York: Aperture, 1979.

Whitehead, Ralph Radcliffe. "A Plea for Manual Work," *Handicraft* 2, no. 3 (June 1903): 66–73.

Zakin, Richard, and Heather Tunis. *American Art Pottery: Pragmatism and Fantasy.* Auburn, N.Y.: Schweinfurth Memorial Art Center, 1982.

Mr. and Mrs. George P. O'Leary
Patricia M. Patterson
Elizabeth Petrie
Mr. and Mrs. Nicholas R. Petry
Mrs. Edward M. Pinsof
Mr. and Mrs. John W. Pitts
Mr. and Mrs. Harvey R. Plonsker
Mr. and Mrs. Lawrence S. Pollock, Jr.
Howard E. Rachofsky
Edward R. Roberts
Mr. and Mrs. Jonathan P. Rosen
Mr. and Mrs. Richard L. Rosenthal
Felice T. Ross
Mr. and Mrs. Lawrence Ruben
Diane Schafer
Mr. and Mrs. Paul C. Schorr, III
Lowell M. Schulman and Dianne Wallace
Adriana Seviroli
Lisa Zenkel Sheldon
Elaine D. Siegel
Mr. and Mrs. Michael R. Sonnenreich
Janet Stern
Dr. and Mrs. Paul Sternberg
Mrs. James G. Stevens
Mr. and Mrs. Harry F. Stimpson, Jr.
Mrs. Richard Swig
Joseph M. Tanenbaum
Rosalie Taubman
Mrs. Norman Tishman
Mr. and Mrs. William B. Troy
Alice S. Warren
Mrs. Robert C. Warren
Mr. and Mrs. Alan Weeden
Mrs. Richard Weil
Mr. and Mrs. Guy A. Weill
Mr. and Mrs. T. Evans Wyckoff

BENEFACTORS CIRCLE

Mr. and Mrs. Steven Ames
Mr. and Mrs. Glenn W. Bailey
Mr. and Mrs. Howard R. Berlin
Ruth Bowman

Mr. and Mrs. James Brice
Melva Bucksbaum
Iris Cantor
Constance R. Caplan
Mr. and Mrs. Donald M. Cox
David L. Davies and John D. Weeden
Mr. and Mrs. Kenneth N. Dayton
Mr. and Mrs. C. Douglas Dillon
Mr. and Mrs. John A. Friede
Mrs. Melville W. Hall
Mr. and Mrs. Lee Hills
Mr. and Mrs. Theodore S. Hochstim
Harry Kahn
Mr. and Mrs. Gilbert H. Kinney
Mr. and Mrs. Richard S. Lane
Mr. and Mrs. Robert E. Linton
Mr. and Mrs. Henry Luce III
Jeanne Lang Mathews
Mr. and Mrs. Frederick R. Mayer
Mrs. C. Blake McDowell, Jr.
Mr. and Mrs. Robert M. Meltzer
Mr. and Mrs. Nicholas Millhouse
Roy R. Neuberger
Mr. and Mrs. Leon B. Polsky
Mr. and Mrs. Milton F. Rosenthal
Barbara Slifka
Ann C. Stephens
Mr. and Mrs. John W. Straus
Mr. and Mrs. David J. Supino
Virginia Ullman
Mr. and Mrs. Michael J. Waldman
Mr. and Mrs. Martin S. Weinberg
Mrs. Keith S. Wellin
Mr. and Mrs. Herbert Wittow

Arthur Wesley Dow and American Arts & Crafts

Coordinated by Michaelyn Mitchell.

Designed by Susan E. Kelly,
Marquand Books, Inc., Seattle.

Edited by Brian Wallis.

Text type digitally set in Mrs Eaves, a typeface
designed by Zuzana Licko in 1996.

Color separating, printing, and binding by
C & C Offset Printing Co., Ltd., Hong Kong.

This catalogue has been published in conjunction
with *Arthur Wesley Dow and American Arts & Crafts,* an exhibition organized by The American Federation of Arts.
Support has been provided by the National Patrons
of the AFA. It is a project of ART ACCESS II, a program of the AFA with major support from the Lila
Wallace–Reader's Digest Fund.

The American Federation of Arts is a nonprofit art
museum service organization that provides traveling
art exhibitions and educational, professional, and
technical support programs developed in collaboration with the museum community. Through these
programs, the AFA seeks to strengthen the ability
of museums to enrich the public's experience and
understanding of art.

EXHIBITION ITINERARY

The Iris and B. Gerald Cantor Center for Visual Arts
Stanford University
Stanford, California
July 13–September 19, 1999

Terra Museum of American Art
Chicago, Illinois
October 8, 1999–January 2, 2000

Georgia O'Keeffe Museum
Santa Fe, New Mexico
  and
Museum of Fine Arts
Santa Fe, New Mexico
March 7–June 18, 2000

Blanden Memorial Art Museum
Fort Dodge, Iowa
July 7–October 1, 2000

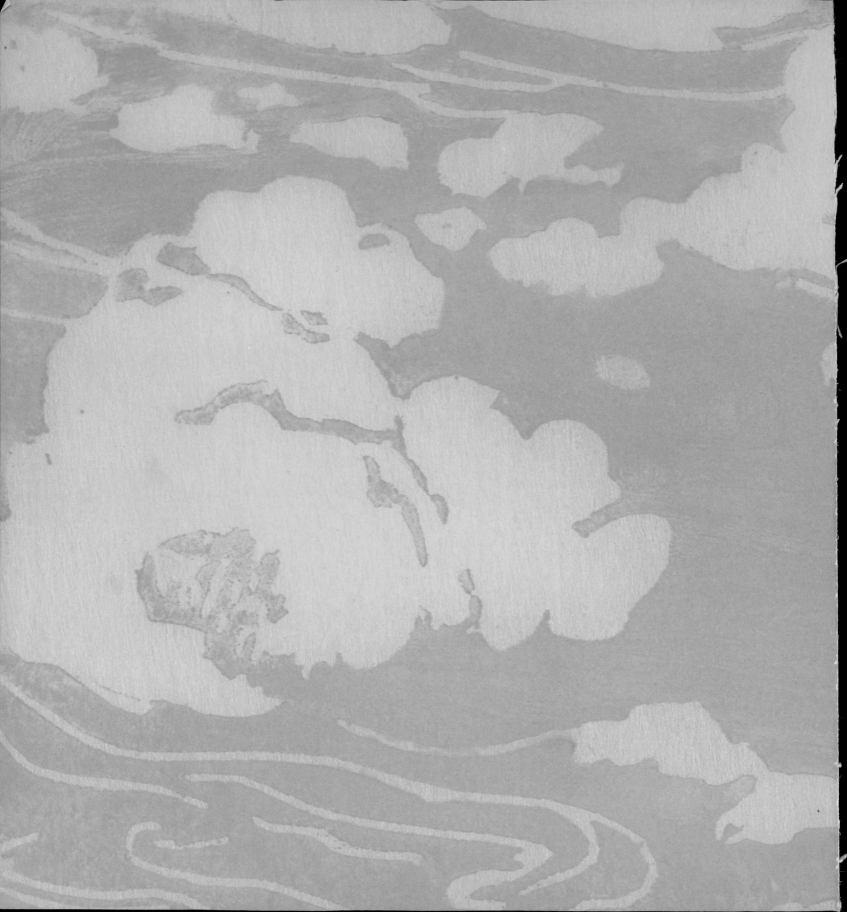